GOD'S DESIGN® FOR LIFE

THE HUMAN BODY

D1476700

1:1

answersingenesis
Petersburg, Kentucky, USA

3RD EDITION | UPDATED, EXPANDED & FULL COLOR

NSWERS IN GENESIS **SCIENCE** BY DEBBIE & RICHARD LAWRENCE

God's Design® for Life is a complete life science curriculum for grades 1–8. The books in this series are designed for use in the Christian school and homeschool, and provide easy-to-use lessons that will encourage children to see God's hand in everything around them.

Third edition
Fifth printing October 2013

ISBN: 1-60092-161-2

Cover design: Brandie Lucas & Diane King
Interior layout: Diane King
Editors: Lori Jaworski, Gary Vaterlaus

The publisher and authors have made every reasonable effort to ensure that the activities recommended in this book are safe when performed as instructed but assume no responsibility for any damage caused or sustained while conducting the experiments and activities. It is the parents', guardians', and/or teachers' responsibility to supervise all recommended activities.

Published by Answers in Genesis, 2800 Bullittsburg Church Rd., Petersburg KY 41080

Printed in China

answersingenesis.org • godsdesignscience.com

PHOTO CREDITS

TABLE OF CONTENTS

UNIT 4 DIGESTION

UNIT 5 HEART & LUNGS

UNIT 6 SKIN & IMMUNITY

WELCOME TO GOD'S DESIGN® FOR LIFE

You are about to start an exciting series of lessons on life science. *God's Design® for Life* consists of three books: *The World of Plants*, *The World of Animals*, and *The Human Body*. Each of these books will give you insight into how God designed and created our world and the things that live in it.

No matter what grade you are in, first through eighth grade, you can use this book.

1st–2nd grade

Read only the "Beginner" section of each lesson, answer the questions at the end of that section, and then do the activity in the ⬤ box (the worksheets will be provided by your teacher).

3rd–5th grade

Skip the "Beginner" section and read the regular part of the lesson. After you read the lesson, do the activity in the ⬤ box and test your understanding by answering the questions in the ◼ box.

6th–8th grade

Skip the "Beginner" section and read the regular part of the lesson. After you read the lesson, do the activity in the ⬤ box and test your understanding by answering the questions in the ◼ box. Also do the "Challenge" section in the ⬤ box. This part of the lesson will challenge you to go beyond just elementary knowledge and do more advanced activities and learn additional interesting information.

Everyone should read the Special Features and do the final project. There are also unit quizzes and a final test to take.

Throughout this book you will see special icons like the one to the right. These icons tell you how the information in the lessons fit into the Seven C's of History: Creation, Corruption, Catastrophe, Confusion, Christ, Cross, Consummation. Your teacher will explain these to you.

Let's get started learning about God's design of our amazing bodies!

UNIT 1

BODY OVERVIEW

◊ **Describe** the function of the major organ systems in the human body.

◊ **Explain** how cells, tissues, organs, and systems are related.

THE CREATION OF LIFE

God created them male and female.

How is man different from the rest of the creatures God created?

BEGINNERS

After God created the earth, plants, sun, moon, stars, and animals, He created man. God took some of the dust from the ground and used His hands to form a man. Then God breathed into the man and made him alive. This first man was named Adam. He was created in God's image and he was created to be God's friend. This was different from God's relationship with the animals. People have a special relationship with God.

God also made a woman for man so that he would not be alone. The first woman was called Eve. Then God told the man and woman to take care of the world that He had made for them.

God created Adam and Eve with wonderful bodies. In this book you are going to learn about the wonderful body that God gave you. God made you special.

- **How did God create the first man, Adam?**

- **In whose image did God create man?**

A fter God created the earth, plants, sun, moon, stars, and animals, He created man. God spoke the entire universe into existence, but He made man out of the dust of the ground with His own hands and breathed life into his body. God created man to be His companion and friend. The special relationship that man has with God is unique in all of creation.

God also made a woman for man so he would not be alone on the earth. God made woman from the side of man and together He charged them with caring for the world He had created.

God gave man and woman wonderful bodies. It has taken scientists thousands of years to even begin to understand the complexity of the human body. Even today, with all of the technology available to us, we have only a small understanding of how everything in the human body really works.

As you study the lessons in this book and learn more about how your body was designed and how it works, remember that God made you special. God wants you to have a relationship with Him. ■

FUN FACT

There are over 6 billion people alive on the earth and each one of them is unique and created in God's image.

SELF-PORTRAIT

Read Genesis 1–2. Discuss how God created humans and why He created them. Then read Psalm 139:13–18. Discuss how God knew each of us even before we were born. Remember that He loves us and has a plan for each of our lives.

Write the words "God Made Me Special" at the top of a sheet of drawing paper. Then using a mirror, try and draw a self portrait.

WHAT DID WE LEARN?

- On which day of creation did God make man?
- In whose image did God create man?
- According to Genesis 1:26, over what were man and woman to rule?

TAKING IT FURTHER

- Since we are created in God's image, how should we treat our bodies?

BODY SYSTEMS

There are eleven recognized systems in the human body. We will be studying eight of those systems in some detail in this book and will briefly look at the other three. On a piece of paper, list as many of the body's systems as you can. Then write a short description of what each system does. Which system do you know the most about? Which system do you know the least about? Which system is the most interesting to you?

OVERVIEW OF THE HUMAN BODY

We are fearfully and wonderfully made!

LESSON 2

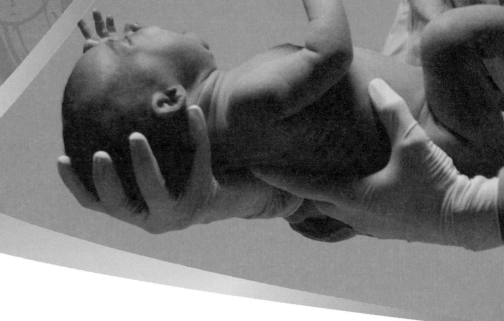

What systems did God give the body to help it accomplish all of the tasks it must perform?

Challenge words:

endocrine system

hormone

excretory system

kidneys

reproductive system

uterus

BEGINNERS

Look in the mirror. What do you see? You see two eyes, two ears, hair, a nose, and a mouth. But do you look just like your mom or dad? Unless you are an identical twin, you don't even look just like your brothers or sisters. Yet your body has all of the same basic parts as everyone else.

You have a heart that moves your blood. You can eat food that gives you energy. You can see, hear, taste, smell, and feel. You also have bones and muscles that help you move. These are all special body parts that God gave each person so that we can run, jump, play, and even clean up our rooms sometimes.

- **What part of your body moves your blood?**

- **What parts of your body help you move?**

- **Who created all the special parts of the human body?**

Perhaps the most amazing of all of God's creations is the human body. It is a complex set of systems all working together. The human body includes systems to move, breathe, eat, think, and feel. These are all wonders of creation. But most animals also have these systems working in their bodies. So what makes people different from animals?

The Bible says that we are created in God's image. We have souls that can relate to God. As we study the wonder of God's creation, remember that we are His handiwork. God designed humans to be very creative like Him. We have been given the ability to think and reason far beyond anything an animal can do. We resemble our Creator and we are separate from the animals.

Some of the remarkable systems that God created for the human body include:

- Skeletal and muscular systems for strength and movement

- Respiratory system for breathing

- Circulatory system for transporting nutrients

- Digestive system for eating

- Nervous system for thinking and feeling

- Skin for protection

- Immune system to fight against disease and other "intruders"

As you learn more about each of these systems, you will marvel at God's creative genius in putting our bodies together. ■

WHAT DID WE LEARN?

- Name as many of the body's systems as you can and describe what each system does.

TAKING IT FURTHER

- Which body systems are used when you walk across a room?

BODY WHEEL

Color each section of the "Body Wheel." Then cut out both circles and connect them with a paper fastener in the center. Turn the top wheel and read the description of each system of the body.

OTHER SYSTEMS

Did you list all eight of the systems on your paper from lesson 1? You are probably somewhat familiar with these body systems, and we will study each system in more detail throughout the remaining lessons in this book. However, there are three other systems that are also important to your body that you might not be as familiar with. We will look at these three systems briefly here. If you want to learn more about these systems, you can study an anatomy book or look in a high school biology book

First is the endocrine system. The endocrine system produces chemical messengers called hormones. These chemicals are produced in special glands and are then secreted into the blood. Hormones control many functions in your body including growth, heart rate, the rate of digestion, waking, and sleeping. You don't have to think about these things. God designed your body to automatically regulate these functions by producing the necessary chemicals.

The second system is the excretory system. This system was designed to remove wastes from the body. Without this system, poisonous substances would build up in your body and eventually kill you. But God designed our bodies to efficiently remove and eliminate unneeded and harmful substances. The main organs of the excretory system are the kidneys, which remove waste substances from the blood, producing urine, which is then eliminated from the body.

Finally, every person has a reproductive system. One of the first commands God gave to Adam and Eve was to be fruitful and multiply. God loves children and designed the human body to be able to create new life. A man's body is designed so that he can become a father. A woman's body is designed to carry the developing child in her womb, called the uterus, until it is ready to be born and then to nourish the new baby with milk from her body. The creation of a new life is a miraculous process designed by God.

Did you include these systems on your list? These are systems that you might not have thought about. Add these systems to your list and include a brief description of each. Every system of your body is necessary and amazing. Enjoy your study of each system and thank God for His wonderful creation.

LEONARDO DA VINCI

1452–1519

Artist, inventor, engineer, genius—which was Leonardo? He was all of these. He was born on April 15, 1452, to Ser Piero da Vinci, a young lawyer, and Caterina, a peasant girl. His name meant "Leonardo, from Vinci." It is believed he was a vegetarian throughout his life. In fact, there are stories that he loved animals so much that he would buy caged animals only to let them go. He studied at home, learning reading, writing, and arithmetic.

When Leonardo was young, his father asked him to paint a round shield. The story goes that Leonardo thought it would be neat to paint a really creepy scene on the shield. He examined all sorts of vermin such as lizards, maggots, and bats to use in the painting. When he showed the shield to his father, his father was so impressed with the realism of the animals, that he knew his son could only be an artist.

Leonardo was successful at nearly everything he did. He was reported to be strikingly handsome with great strength. He also had a fine singing voice. He quickly learned to play the lyre, and he would sing and beautifully improvise with it. But good looks, strength, and musical talent were just the beginning. He was most gifted in art and science.

In 1469, at the age of 17, Leonardo and his father moved to Florence, Italy where he worked under the master artist, Verrocchio. It soon became apparent that his skills surpassed that of his teacher's. In 1472 Leonardo joined the painter's guild of Florence where he had contact with many other great Florentine artists. At this time, Leonardo started working for himself. Not only was he doing paintings, he was also sketching water pumps, military weapons, and other machines. One of the more unusual characteristics about Leonardo was that he was not only left-handed, which is not too uncommon, but he wrote many of his papers and works from right to left and backwards. Many of his notes can only be read in a mirror.

In 1482 the Duke of Milan hired Leonardo as a painter and engineer. During his 17 years under the duke, he completed six paintings and worked as an adviser on architecture, fortifications, military matters, hydraulics, and mechanical engineering. In 1489 Leonardo did some of his earliest drawings of human anatomy, and even though most of his drawings were completely wrong, he produced extremely accurate cross-sectional representations of the skull. By

1495 Leonardo felt he had achieved his goal in understanding the human anatomy and he abandoned his work in this area for eight years.

During his time with the duke, Leonardo spent many hours studying geometry. This took time away from his painting. But he wrote a book on the elementary theory of mechanics. It was also during his time under the duke that he started exploring the possibility of constructing a telescope, looked into flying machines, designed advanced weapons, including tanks and other vehicles for war, and designed submarines. During this period, Leonardo achieved new heights of scientific thought.

When the Duke of Milan died, his son wanted Leonardo to make a bronze sculpture of his father on horseback. The sculpture was to be four times bigger than life size and weigh about 80 tons. But this task proved too challenging even for Leonardo. Leonardo studied for years, developing new casting methods, but when the French invaded, he had only been successful in building a 22-foot clay model. He left Florence in 1499 when the French soldiers used the model for target practice.

Leonardo spent the next few years traveling through southern Europe. From 1502 to 1503 he worked as a military engineer for Cesare Borgia. After this, he returned to Florence for three years. It was during this time he painted what is perhaps his most famous work, the "Mona Lisa." In 1504, Leonardo received word of his father's death. His father's estate went to his half brothers and sisters, so he left Florence for Milan only to return the following year to fight for his uncle's estate, which he eventually inherited.

In the winter of 1507–1508 his interest in the human anatomy was revived when he witnessed an old man die. The man claimed to be one hundred years old. The old man told Leonardo before dying that he felt fine, only weaker.

Leonardo wanted to know how this man could have such a peaceful death, so he studied this man's anatomy and found an absence of fat. This study allowed Leonardo to complete the most detailed records of a single subject. During his lifetime, Leonardo made hundreds of sketches of the human body.

In 1509 Leonardo returned to Milan and spent time on other scientific studies including a project to change the course of the Abba River. From 1510 to 1513 he concentrated on the study of human anatomy and developed a new way to do science. The old way was to interpret everything with what you already knew; the new method was to first observe and then see if it fit with what you understood. During this time, Leonardo did some of his most famous anatomical drawings—one of them being the "Embryo in the Womb," which is still found in some medical textbooks today.

In 1513 Leonardo went to Rome under the protection of Giuliano de Medici, the brother of Pope Leo X. He had a workshop and undertook a variety of projects for the Pope. He was also able to continue his studies in human anatomy. However, the Pope would not allow him to dissect any cadavers.

Following the death of Giuliano de Medici, Francis I of France offered Leonardo the position of Premier Painter, Engineer, and Architect of the King. Leonardo accepted the position and went to work for the king of France where he lived in a house near the royal chateau at Amboise. He worked for King Francis until his death, and legend has it that when he died in 1519, King Francis was at his side, cradling Leonardo's head in his arms. Leonardo da Vinci was buried in the cloister of San Fiorentino in Amboise, France. The world will remember him as a painter, architect, engineer, and scientist with one of the brightest minds of the Middle Ages.

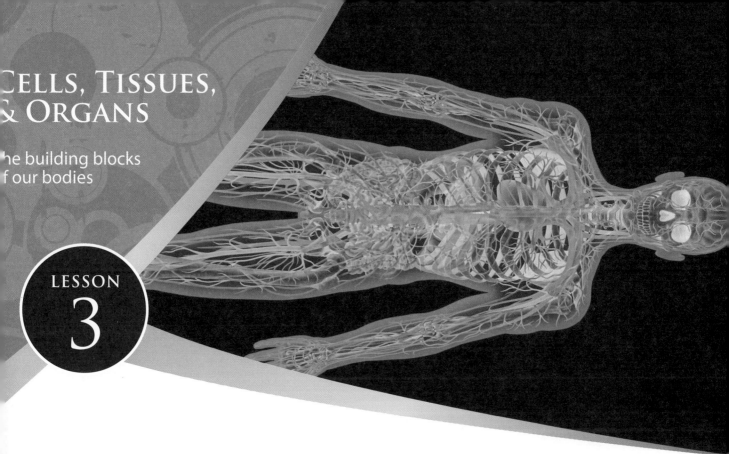

CELLS, TISSUES, & ORGANS

The building blocks of our bodies

How are organs related to cells?

Words to know:

cell

tissue

organ

cell membrane

nucleus

cytoplasm

mitochondria

vacuole

Challenge words:

muscle tissue

nerve tissue

epithelial tissue

connective tissue

BEGINNERS

Have you ever played with a model made from small connecting blocks? It may be a space ship or a building. After you play with it you can take it apart and look at each piece. Some pieces might be red, others might be yellow or white. Some pieces might be square or rectangular, while others are round or unusually shaped. When you look at the pieces by themselves, they don't look much like the final product, but when they are put together in a certain way, they become something special.

Your body is the same way. It is made up of many different parts that may not look like much by themselves, but when they are all put together they become you! The smallest parts of your body, the building blocks, are called **cells**. A group of cells can be put together to form a **tissue**, just like a group of blocks can form a wall. Many tissues can be put together to make an **organ**, just like several walls can make a building. We will be learning about many of the organs in your body and what each organ does as we go through the rest of the lessons in this book. For today, remember that your body is made up of smaller pieces that work together.

• **What are the smallest parts of your body called?**

• **What do these parts make when they are put together?**

The systems of the human body begin with cells. **Cells** are the smallest part of the human body that can function on their own. Cells are essentially the building blocks of your body. Many cells working together form a **tissue**, and many tissues working together form an **organ**. Each system is comprised of cells, tissues, and organs all working together to perform a certain function.

Although various kinds of cells may look different, they all have some similar features. All cells have a **cell membrane**, which surrounds and protects the rest of the cell, somewhat like your skin. Also, every cell has a **nucleus**, which functions as the brain of the cell. Cells are filled with a liquid called **cytoplasm**, which allows the other parts of the cell to move around inside the cell. All cells have **mitochondria**, which convert organic material into energy for the cell. And finally, cells have **vacuoles**,

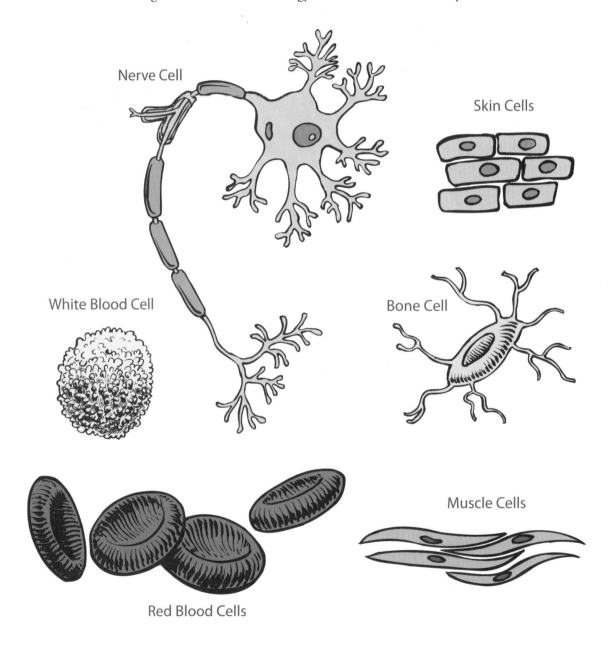

Nerve Cell

Skin Cells

White Blood Cell

Bone Cell

Muscle Cells

Red Blood Cells

BODY CELLS

Complete the "Body Cells" worksheet. Use the pictures on the previous page as a guide.

which store food or any variety of nutrients a cell might need to survive. They even store waste products so the rest of the cell is protected from contamination.

Even though all cells have these common characteristics, the cells in each system are specially designed for their jobs. Red blood cells, which move throughout the body inside the blood vessels, are round and smooth. They are shaped like disks, or little lifesavers. Their cell membrane is designed to allow oxygen and carbon dioxide to pass through. White blood cells look like white balls but can change their shape to surround germs that get inside the body. Skin cells are rectangular and fit together to keep germs on the outside and moisture on the inside of the body.

Muscle cells are long and stretchy, allowing them to expand and contract so our bodies can move. Bone cells crisscross to make strong structures. Nerve cells have an irregular shape that allows signals to move efficiently throughout the body. This lets the brain "talk" to all parts of the body very quickly. A nerve cell can be over one yard (1 m) long. God designed each cell to look and act differently based on its function in the body.

The cells, or building blocks, work together to make tissues and the tissues work together to make organs such as muscles, lungs, the brain, and your skin. We group these organs together into systems by what they do for us. For example, the heart and blood work together to take oxygen and nutrients to every part of the body, so we call them the circulatory system. The brain, spinal cord, and all of our nerves work together to communicate messages to the body, so we group them together and call them the nervous system. We will study each system of the human body separately to better understand its function. ■

WHAT DID WE LEARN?

- What is the function of each of the following kinds of cells: skin cells, red blood cells, white blood cells, bone cells, nerve cells, and muscle cells?

TAKING IT FURTHER

- How has God uniquely designed red blood cells to transport oxygen?
- How are nerve cells specially designed to carry signals?
- How did God design skin cells to perform their special functions?
- With all these cells working together, what do you think is the largest organ in the body?

TISSUE TYPES

The human body contains many organs and tissues. These tissues are classified into four different categories.

- **Muscle tissue** is designed to contract. Its main function is movement.

- **Nerve tissue** controls body activities and coordinates functions.

- **Epithelial tissue** lines all of your body parts, both inside and out. Epithelial tissue secretes liquid that lubricates all the parts of your body to reduce friction as your body parts move. It also covers and protects each part of your body.

- **Connective tissue** holds your body together. Many connective tissues are solid; however, blood and lymph are considered connective tissues even though they are liquids because they connect all of the parts of the body together as they circulate throughout the body.

Based on what you just learned about the different kinds of tissues, identify which type of tissue each of the following body parts belongs to. Some of these are tricky so don't be surprised if you get some wrong.

- Skin
- Muscles
- Tendons
- Lining of the mouth
- Brain
- Inside of lungs
- Fat
- Bones

UNIT 2

BONES & MUSCLES

◊ **Identify** the major bones of the body.

◊ **Describe** the relationship between muscles and bones.

◊ **Distinguish** between voluntary and involuntary muscles.

THE SKELETAL SYSTEM

Structure and strength

What allows bones to move?

Words to know:

skeletal system

muscular system

tendon

cartilage

Challenge words:

axial skeleton

appendicular skeleton

BEGINNERS

Are you as tall as your mother or father? Probably not yet. One of the main things that determines your height is the length of the bones in your legs. Compare how long your leg bones are to your mother's leg bones. If her leg bones are longer than yours, she is probably taller than you are.

The bones in your body also determine the general size and shape of your body. If your shoulder bones and hips are wide, you will be wider than someone with narrow bones.

Your bones give you strength and help you move, too. When you push against your bones they do not bend. You have special areas between the bones that bend, but the bones themselves to not bend. Wiggle your fingers and watch the bones move. Aren't you glad God gave you bones?

• **What are three things that bones do for you?**

• **Do bones bend?**

Wh4at gives the human body its strength, shape, and form? Two systems work together to do this: the skeletal and muscular systems. The **skeletal system** gives the body strength and determines its general size and shape. The **muscular system** helps the bones to move and gives us our general appearance.

The adult human body has 206 bones. Eighty bones are in the head, ribs, and spine; sixty bones are in the hands and feet; sixty bones are in the legs and arms; four bones make up the shoulder girdle; and two bones make up the pelvic girdle. Bones are made mostly from calcium and make up approximately 20% of your body weight. Bones are very strong—as strong as reinforced concrete!

Some of the jobs performed by your bones include:

- providing structure, strength, and protection to vital organs

- producing blood cells (about 2 million red blood cells are produced inside your bones every second!)

- storing calcium and phosphorous

Bones are connected to muscles by cord-like structures called **tendons**. This allows the muscles to move the bones when the muscles contract. **Cartilage** is a smooth material, which forms a cushion between bones where they meet so they do not rub against each other. Cartilage also connects the ribs to the sternum, which is the vertical bone in the center of your chest. Without your skeletal system, you would be a squishy lump or just a bag of flesh. ■

FUN FACT

Babies actually have more bones than adults. The bones in a baby's head are not fused like they are in an adult. This allows for easier birth. As the child grows, the bones grow and fuse together, so an adult actually has fewer separate bones than a newborn baby.

SANDY SKELETON

Cut out and assemble "Sandy Skeleton." It is not necessary for younger children to cut exactly on the lines in order to put the skeleton together.

WHAT DID WE LEARN?

- What are three jobs that bones perform?
- How are muscles connected to bones?
- What keeps bones from rubbing against each other at the joints?
- How many bones does an adult human have?
- What is the main mineral in bones?

TAKING IT FURTHER

- What do you think is the largest bone in the body?
- Why does this bone need to be so large?
- What do you think are the smallest bones in the body?

YOUR SKELETON

The skeletal system is divided into two broad categories called the axial skeleton and the appendicular skeleton. The **axial skeleton** (below right) consists of all the bones in the skull, face, neck, spine, sternum, and ribs. These are the bones that are generally in the center part of your body. The axial skeleton provides protection to all your vital organs such as your brain, heart, and lungs. There are 80 bones in the axial skeleton.

The **appendicular skeleton** (below left) consists of all the bones in your arms, legs, hips, shoulders, hands, and feet. These are the bones that provide strength, form, and mobility. There are 126 bones in the appendicular skeleton.

The bones in your spine are called vertebrae and between each vertebra there is a cushioning pad made of cartilage. As you sleep at night, these cartilage pads absorb a small amount of water. This causes your spine to expand slightly. But as you walk around all day, gravity pulls down on your body and some of the water is squeezed out of the cartilage pads and they compress. This means that you are probably slightly shorter at night than you are first thing in the morning. Test this to find out how much your height changes. Carefully measure your height first thing in the morning. Then, measure your height again just before you go to bed and see if you notice a difference.

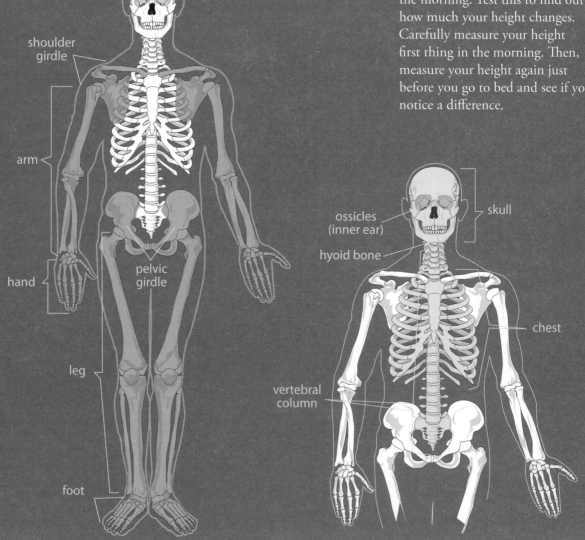

shoulder girdle

arm

hand

pelvic girdle

leg

foot

ossicles (inner ear)

hyoid bone

vertebral column

skull

chest

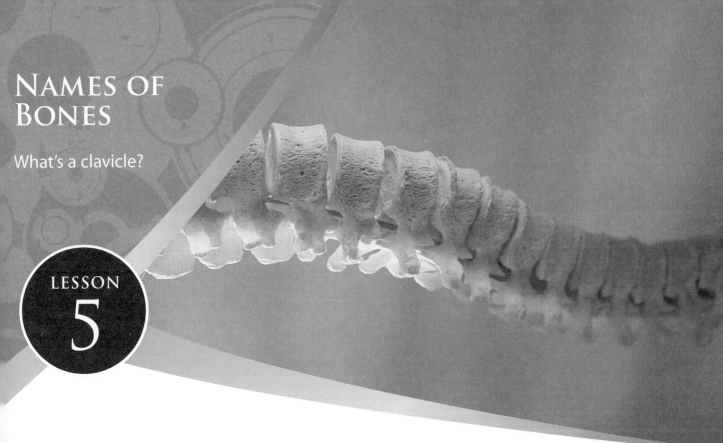

NAMES OF BONES

What's a clavicle?

LESSON 5

BEGINNERS

Your body has 206 bones. Isn't that amazing? And each bone has a special name. Some of these names sound kind of funny. Some of the bones in your body are called **carpals** and others are called **phalanges**. One is even called your **humerus**. But we are not going to have you memorize all 206 names. It would be fun however to memorize the names of a few of the bones in your body.

Let's start with the bones on the top of your head. Together they make up your skull, or **cranium**. Below that is the bone that opens and closes your mouth. You may call it your jawbone, but scientists call it your **mandible**. Another bone is the bone on the front of your knee. It is called a kneecap, but if you want to learn the scientific name, it is called the **patella**. Finally, the big bone in your upper leg is called the **femur**. See how many of these names you can remember. If you are really interested in learning bone names, you can look at an anatomy book to see the scientific names of even more bones.

- How many bones do you have in your body?
- What is the bone on the top of your head called?
- What is the name of the bone that opens and closes your mouth?
- What is the name of the bone at the front of your knee?
- What is the name of the long bone in the top of your leg?

M any of the bones in our bodies have familiar names and others seem peculiar. It is fun to learn the names of the bones in the body, and it is important. Knowing the names of bones will help you better understand and appreciate what your bones do. Look in an anatomy book and locate the bones mentioned below as you read about them.

Your skull is called your **cranium**. The bones in your spine are called **vertebrae**. Your **mandible** is your jawbone. Your **clavicle** is also called your collarbone. **Phalanges** are the bones in your fingers and toes. Your **patella** is your kneecap. The **sternum** is the vertical bone in the middle of your chest that is connected to some of your ribs. **Carpals** and **metacarpals** can be found in your hands and wrists, while the **malleus**, **incus**, and **stapes** (also called the hammer, anvil, and stirrup) are found in your ear. The **ulna**, **radius**, and **humerus** are your arm bones and the **femur**, **fibula**, and **tibia** are your leg bones. Finally, your shoulder blades are called **scapulas**. Did you find all of these bones in your anatomy book?

If you can remember the names of these bones, you will know most of the major bones in your body. Use your anatomy book to review the names of these bones every day until you have them memorized.

You can also use some of these sayings to help you remember the names of some of your bones:

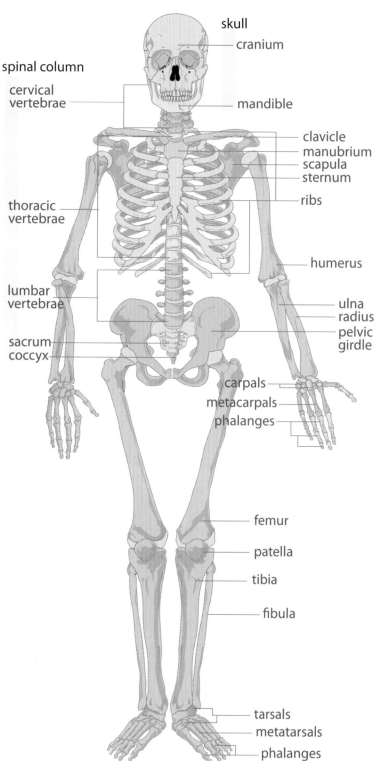

skull
cranium
spinal column
cervical vertebrae
mandible
clavicle
manubrium
scapula
sternum
ribs
thoracic vertebrae
humerus
lumbar vertebrae
ulna
radius
pelvic girdle
sacrum
coccyx
carpals
metacarpals
phalanges
femur
patella
tibia
fibula
tarsals
metatarsals
phalanges

LABEL THOSE BONES

Put on a swimming suit and write the names of bones where they are located on your body with a washable gel pen. You can write many of the names on yourself or you can write on a friend or sibling and let them write on you. If a washable gel pen is not available, you can write the names on sticky notes and stick them on your body.

After you are done labeling your bones, make up a bone rap or song.

Bones & Muscles

- If you bump your head you can crack your cranium.
- Your humerus is just above your funny bone.
- The patella caps off your knee.
- Put your hand on your jaw to "handible" your mandible.
- I keep my lungs in a cage: my rib cage.

Now make up your own sayings to help you remember the names of other bones. ■

WHAT DID WE LEARN?

- Review the names of the bones by pointing to each bone as you name it.
- Is your cranium above or below your mandible?
- What is moving if you wiggle your phalanges?

TAKING IT FURTHER

- What happens if you cross your legs and gently hit just below your patella?
- Why do we have Latin names for body parts?

WHAT'S MY NAME?

Complete the "What's My Name?" worksheet.

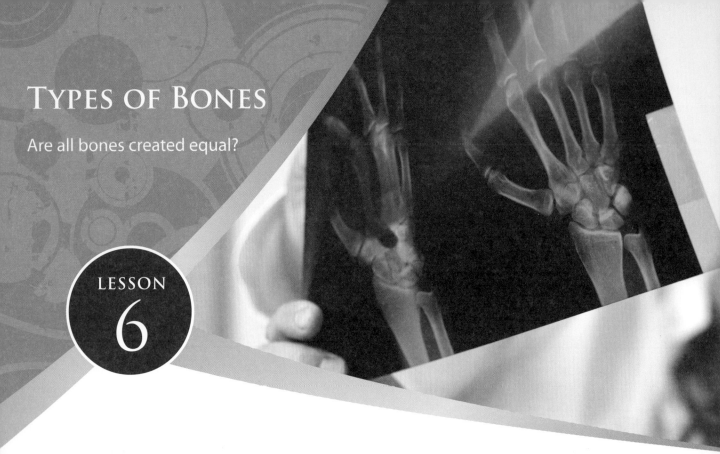

TYPES OF BONES

Are all bones created equal?

LESSON 6

How is a rib different from a femur?

Words to know:

short bones

long bones

flat bones

irregular bones

Challenge words:

fracture

simple fracture

compound fracture

collagen

BEGINNERS

Today we are going to take another look at the bones in your body. Do all the bones look alike? No, some of the bones are longer and some are shorter than others. Does your jawbone have the same shape as a rib? No. God has designed each bone for a special purpose so each bone has a special shape and size.

The bones in your fingers and toes are **short bones**. Shorter bones can move in many different ways, which helps you be able to pick things up and to walk smoothly. Some bones are long like the ones in your arms and legs. These **long bones** give you strength. Your ribs are flat with a little bit of a curve. These **flat bones** are designed to protect the softer parts of your body like your lungs and your heart. Finally, some bones, like your jawbone, are unusually shaped, yet they are made just right for the job that they do. See how many different shapes of bones you can find.

• **What are three different shapes of bones in your body?**

Bones are classified into four types by their shapes. There are long bones, short bones, flat bones, and irregular bones. Leg and arm bones are **long bones**. These are the bones that give you your height and bear most of your weight. Also, these long bones are factories for new red blood cells that are produced in the marrow in the center of the bones. Approximately 2 million red blood cells are produced each second inside the long bones. Long bones also produce many of the white blood cells and platelets in your blood (we'll learn about these in lesson 26).

Short bones are the ones in your fingers, toes, hands, and feet. They give us dexterity and flexibility in walking and allow us to do most of the functions we do each day. Short bones include carpals and metacarpals, tarsals and metatarsals, as well as phalanges.

Flat bones include the shoulder blades (scapula), skull (cranium), ribs, and pelvis. Their primary function is the protection of vital organs. These bones protect the brain, heart, lungs, and other internal organs.

All other bones are **irregular bones** because they all have different shapes. Some of the irregular bones include the vertebrae and facial bones. The vertebrae are round bones that are hollow in the center. Their primary function is to protect the spinal cord. There are 26 individual bones stacked on top of each other in a curved column. This design allows us to easily bend and move in many different ways.

Facial bones give our faces form and structure. Along with the facial muscles and fat, these bones help people identify you as the unique person you are.

Each type of bone has a special function and performs in a way to make the human body one of God's greatest creations. ■

FUN FACT

Humans and giraffes have the same number of bones in their necks. A giraffe's neck vertebrae are just much, much longer.

SIMON SAYS

Review the names of the major bones using an anatomy book or Sandy Skeleton. Then take turns playing "Simon Says" with someone, asking each other to point to specific bones using their scientific names.

WHAT DID WE LEARN?

- Which bones are designed mainly for protection of internal organs?
- Which type of bones helps determine what your face will look like?
- Which type of bones works closely with your circulatory system to replace old blood cells?

TAKING IT FURTHER

- Why are the long bones filled with marrow and not solid?
- What is the advantage of having so many small bones in your hands?

BROKEN BONES

Bones are very strong—stronger than reinforced concrete. But sometimes an unusual force can cause a bone to break. A break in a bone is called a fracture. Most broken bones are classified as simple fractures. This means that the bones remain inside the body after they are broken. However, occasionally the broken bone will pierce the skin. This is classified as a compound fracture.

When a bone breaks, the parts must be realigned and held in place while the fracture heals. God designed bones so that they are very efficient at repairing themselves. Some cells clot the broken blood vessels right away to control bleeding. Then new blood vessels form quickly to supply the area with nutrients and raw materials for constructing new bone.

Next, special bone cells fill in the break with cartilage. This cartilage

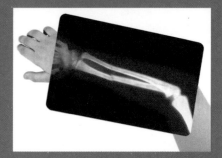

is slowly replaced with new bone cells. This process can take several weeks, but once it is complete, the bone may actually be stronger than it was before the break.

Purpose: To understand what gives bones their strength

Materials: two cleaned chicken leg bones, cup, vinegar

Procedure:

1. Place one chicken leg bone in a cup and cover it with vinegar. What do you see happening?

2. Cover the cup so the vinegar does not evaporate.

3. Set the second bone next to the cup in the open air.

4. After three or four days, compare the bones. The bone that was not in the vinegar should be very dry.

5. Try to break the bone that was in the air. It should break easily. Examine the break. Try to place the bone back together. What would have to happen to repair the break? God has designed chicken bodies to be able to repair broken bones too.

6. Now examine the bone from the vinegar. How does it feel?

7. Try to break this bone. What happened?

Conclusion: The bone that was in the vinegar should be very flexible and should bend but not break. The vinegar has chemically reacted with the calcium in the bone leaving behind only the collagen. Collagen is a flexible protein that builds the structure of the bone. Without the calcium, however, the bone is not strong. Your bones need calcium, too, so it is important to eat foods with calcium so your bones will be strong. A few foods that contain a lot of calcium are milk, cheese, soy products, beans, almonds, and orange juice.

JOINTS

Connections are important

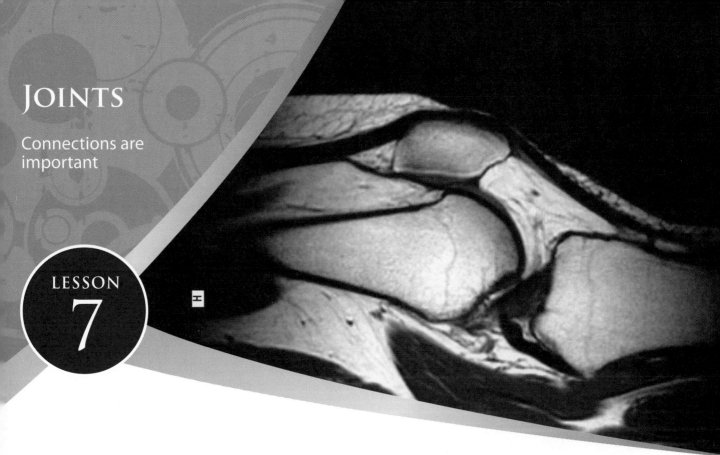

How is your knee similar to a door?

Words to know:

hinge joint

ball and socket joint

pivot joint

ellipsoid joint

saddle joint

gliding joint

Challenge words:

ligament

synovial fluid

BEGINNERS

How many different ways can you wiggle your fingers? What directions can you move your head? How can you move your legs? Your different body parts move in many directions because of the joints in your body. Joints are where two bones come together.

Some joints allow the bones to only bend in one direction. Your fingers, but not your thumbs, have this kind of joint. They can bend forward and back up but cannot bend side to side. Knees bend this way, too. The joints in your thumbs allow you to move them around in many more ways than your other fingers so you can hold on to things.

Your shoulder joints are even more flexible. You can move your shoulders in nearly every direction. God didn't make fingers move the way that shoulders do because they don't need to be able to twist all around in order to pick things up. But shoulders need to be more flexible so we can reach around and scratch our backs, and do many other things too. Necks rotate side to side so you can see things around you. God knew exactly what He was doing when he designed our joints.

- What is a joint?

- How does your knee joint move?

- How does your neck joint move?

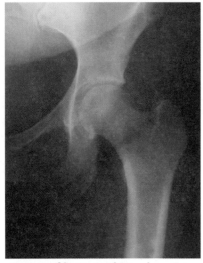

X-ray of human hip, showing the ball and socket joint

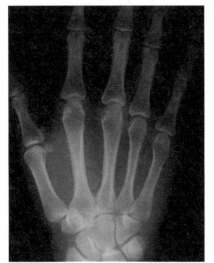

X-ray of human hand, showing the finger hinge joints

All the bones in your body are connected together at joints. Different types of joints provide different movement. A few joints in the cranium are immovable and some joints, such as the vertebrae, are only slightly moveable. But most joints are freely moveable. This is what makes the body so flexible and allows humans to do so much.

There are 6 types of joints found in the body.

- **Hinge joint**: Knees and fingers are hinge joints. They can move in one plane, or back and forth only.

- **Ball and socket joint**: Hips and shoulders are ball and socket joints. They can move in two planes which means they can rotate in place.

- **Pivot joint**: Your neck is a pivot joint. This means it rotates around a fixed point.

- **Ellipsoid joint**: You find ellipsoid joints where fingers connect to the hand. These joints move in two directions without rotating. Your fingers can move up and down and side to side but cannot rotate.

- **Saddle joint**: Where your thumb connects to your hand is a saddle joint. Your thumb moves in two directions but the joint is shaped like a horse's saddle, giving it more flexibility than your fingers.

- **Gliding joint**: Hand bones form gliding joints. One bone slips or glides over another.

God designed each joint for its specific function. He did not create fingers that can turn in any direction because fingers would not work as well that way. It would be harder to pick things up if fingers bent backwards. But God designed your shoulders to move in nearly every direction so you could reach all the things you need to reach, including that itch in the middle of your back. ■

SCAVENGER HUNT

Search your house for examples of different types of joints. Try and identify the different types of joints you find.

Examples could be:

- door hinges

- sliding doors
- joints in pets
- LEGO® pieces
- nut crackers
- pliers, or other tools

This list is just to get you started. You will be amazed at how many different joints there are around your house.

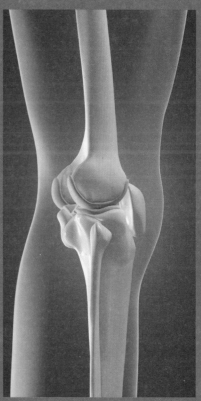

WHAT DID WE LEARN?

- What was the most common joint found around your house?

TAKING IT FURTHER

- Which came first, the joints in the body or the joints in your house?
- Why do you need so many different kinds of joints in your body?

AMAZING JOINTS

A joint is much more than just the point where two bones come together. In order for a joint to work properly, the bones must be held in place, yet be able to move freely. This sounds like an impossible task, yet God designed strong flexible cords called ligaments to hold the bones in place while allowing them to move within the joint.

Also, the bones cannot rub against each other when they move, or they would quickly wear out. To prevent this, the ends of bones are covered with a slippery substance called cartilage. Cartilage is tough but allows the bones to slide easily. The cartilage is also coated with a slippery fluid that keeps things moving smoothly. This substance is called synovial fluid. The ligaments completely encase the joint, which not only holds the bones in place, but also holds the synovial fluid inside the joint. All of these things work together to hold the bones together.

Illustration of a human knee showing the cartilage in blue

Purpose: To build a model joint

Materials: two wooden pencils, rubber bands, tacks

Procedure:

1. Place two wooden pencils end to end. These represent two bones.

2. Attach several wide rubber bands across the "joint" using tacks or small nails to hold the "bones" together. The rubber bands are like the ligaments that hold your joints together.

3. See if you can move your pencil joint around and still keep the pencils close together.

THE MUSCULAR SYSTEM

Making it move

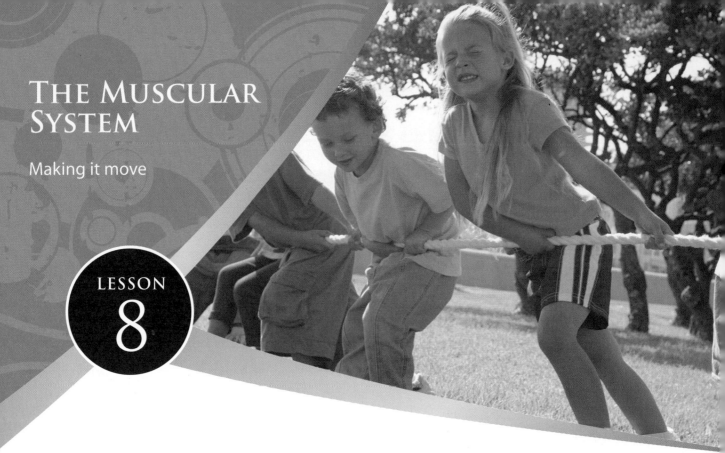

What pairs of muscles allow you to swing a hammer?

Words to know:

muscular system

bicep

tricep

pectoral

trapezius

gluteus maximus

diaphragm

BEGINNERS

Put your right hand on the upper part of your left arm. Can you feel the big muscle there? See if you can make the muscle feel hard by bending your arm. Now stretch out your arm. How does the muscle feel now? It should feel softer and smaller.

Muscles are connected to your bones so you can move your bones. Without muscles you would be like a statue, unable to move at all. Muscles also give your body some of its shape. Your bones give you height and your general shape, but the muscles under the skin really make you look the way you do.

Do you remember learning the names of some of the bones in your body? You should remember where your cranium (skull), mandible (jawbone), patella (kneecap), and femur (thigh bone) are. Today, we are going to learn the names of a few muscles. The big muscle in your arm is called the **bicep**. On the back of your arm, on the opposite side from the bicep, is the **tricep**. These two muscles work together to bend and straighten your arm. One of the most important muscles is the muscle in your chest below your lungs. This muscle is called your **diaphragm**, and it helps you breathe by making your chest get bigger to draw in air.

- **What is the main job of your muscles?**

- **What are the names of the muscles in your upper arm?**

- **What does your diaphragm muscle do?**

Do you like to run and jump? Do you like to play soccer or the piano? Then be glad for your muscular and skeletal systems. The **muscular system** works together with the skeleton to allow us to move our bodies. The muscles are attached to the bones by cords called tendons. When a muscle contracts, it gets smaller and pulls the bone. For example, to bend your arm, the muscle on the front of your arm above the elbow (called a bicep) contracts, causing your arm to bend.

But muscles cannot stretch or "uncontract" by themselves. After moving a bone, the muscle relaxes but does not stretch out again. Another muscle on the other side of the bone must contract to move the bone and stretch the first muscle out again. Muscles work together in pairs. There are pairs of muscles in many different locations all over your body allowing you to move in many different directions.

It is important to learn the names of some of the muscles. Some of the more important muscles include **biceps** and **triceps** in your upper arm, **pectoral** muscles in your upper chest, **trapezius** muscles in your upper back and shoulders, and the **gluteus maximus** muscles in your rear. One very specialized muscle is the **diaphragm** below your lungs. This muscle contracts to expand your chest cavity and allow air to enter your lungs.

Look at the diagrams here or in an anatomy book to see where all of these muscles are found in the body. There are also many other muscles in your body that you can learn about as well.

Your muscles make up about 40 percent of your body weight. They are also the part of your body that gives it most of its shape. The muscles in your face, along with a layer of fat, determine what your face looks like. The muscles in your face also help you express feelings by changing the expression on your face. ■

FUN FACT

It takes more muscles to frown than to smile. So smile—it's easier.

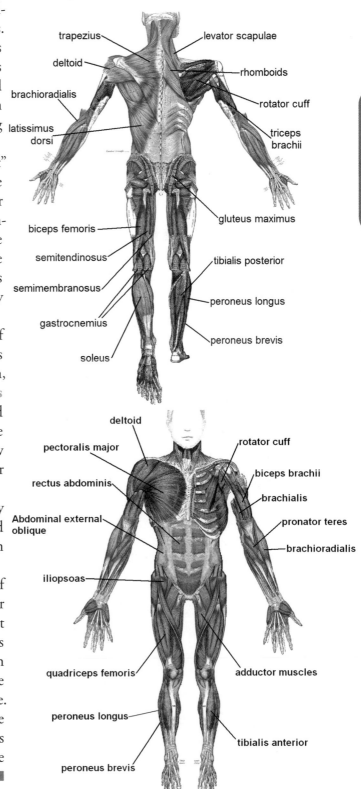

trapezius
levator scapulae
deltoid
rhomboids
brachioradialis
rotator cuff
latissimus dorsi
triceps brachii
gluteus maximus
biceps femoris
semitendinosus
tibialis posterior
semimembranosus
peroneus longus
gastrocnemius
peroneus brevis
soleus

deltoid
pectoralis major
rotator cuff
rectus abdominis
biceps brachii
brachialis
Abdominal external oblique
pronator teres
brachioradialis
iliopsoas
quadriceps femoris
adductor muscles
peroneus longus
tibialis anterior
peroneus brevis

FIND THE PAIRS

Purpose: To discover muscle pairs on your body

Materials: none

Procedure:

1. Stretch out your left arm and feel the bicep. It should feel long and stretched.

2. Now feel the back side of your arm. Your tricep will feel hard.

3. Next, bend your arm and feel the muscles again. Now the bicep should feel shorter and harder and the tricep should feel long and stretched.

Try to discover as many other pairs of muscles as possible. Try bending your legs, swinging a straight leg, making a fist, and smiling and frowning. Not all muscle pairs are easily identifiable. Smiling and frowning require many muscles, not just a single pair of muscles.

WHAT DID WE LEARN?

- How does a contracted muscle feel?
- How does a muscle get stretched?

TAKING IT FURTHER

- How does a muscle know when to contract?
- How does your face express emotion?

MUSCLE JOBS

You learned in lesson 3 that muscle cells expand and contract. These special cells are what give muscles their strength and flexibility. Each cell contracts when it receives an impulse from the nerve that is attached to it. The cells in most muscle tissue are lined up in parallel rows so they can all contract together in the same direction. This gives muscles a striped appearance.

Many muscles are designed to move bones, but muscles have other jobs too. You probably already know that your heart is a muscle but it was not designed to moves bones; it was designed to move blood. Your heart pumps blood throughout your whole body. However, you may not know that muscles that move bones, such as your leg muscles, also help move the blood in your legs. When your leg muscles contract they squeeze the veins in you legs, helping to push the blood back toward your heart. You may have heard that exercise is good for your circulation. This is true because the movement of your muscles helps move the blood through the blood vessels.

Other muscles help move your food through your digestive system. Beginning in your throat, down your esophagus, in your stomach, and throughout your intestines, muscles contract and expand to move your latest meal through the digestive process. Finally, muscles in your arms and legs help move lymph fluid throughout your body, in the same way they help move blood. You will learn more about the lymph system in lesson 32.

Use a magnifying glass to closely examine a piece of raw steak. Look for parallel lines of meat. These are the muscle tissues that are lined up parallel to allow the muscles to contract in a strong way.

DIFFERENT TYPES OF MUSCLES

aren't they all the same?

LESSON
9

How are the muscles in your heart different from the muscles in your digestive tract?

Words to know:

voluntary muscles

involuntary muscles

smooth muscles

Challenge words:

striated muscle tissue

cardiac muscle tissue

smooth muscle tissue

BEGINNERS

Practice using your muscles. Move your arms and legs. When you walk, run, or ride your bike you are using your muscles. You can blink your eyes, stick out your tongue, or make a funny face. These activities will use your muscles too. This is what they were made for. Your muscles get bigger and stronger the more you use them. If you exercise and use your muscles every day your body will be healthier and you will be stronger.

Most muscles only move when you think about moving them, like when you move your arm or leg. But some muscles work without you even knowing about them. One of these muscles is your heart. It beats many times every minute when you are awake and when you are asleep. When you exercise, your heart beats faster, but you don't have to think about it, your body takes care of it automatically.

You also have muscles in your stomach to move the food around and to push it through your digestive system. You even have muscles to help you breathe. Remember how we learned about the diaphragm? This muscle works to help you breathe even when you are asleep. You don't even have to think about it.

- How can you make your muscles stronger?
- How do you make most muscles move?
- What are some muscles that move without you having to think about it?

The muscles we learned about in the last lesson are ones that move when your brain tells them to. You can decide to make them move and they do. They are called **voluntary muscles**. But the body has other muscles that move without you having to think about it. These are called **involuntary muscles**. One of these muscles, your heart, keeps your blood moving around your body. It automatically contracts and relaxes continuously whether you are awake or asleep. Your diaphragm muscle, which expands your chest cavity so you can breathe, is an involuntary muscle that you can also control to a small extent.

Other involuntary muscles are called **smooth muscles**. These muscles line your digestive tract and automatically move the food through your intestines. Involuntary muscles are vital to keeping you healthy and keeping your body functioning. You have enough to think about without having to think about digesting your food or making your heart beat.

Muscles play such an important part in your body that you need to take good care of them. To have healthy muscles you must eat right and exercise. Muscles are built with nutrients called proteins, so when you eat meat and dried beans, or drink milk, you are giving your body foods that help to build muscle.

It is important to stretch your muscles before you exercise.

MUSCLE MEMORY EXERCISES

Your muscles and your brain work together to help you move and do activities. If you do something over and over again, your brain and your muscles learn to do it very efficiently. Practice the following activities every day for three days. You will notice that your muscles "gain a memory" and improve from the first time to the last time.

Activity 1: Have someone use a stopwatch and time how long you can stand on one foot. You should be able to stand longer each day.

Activity 2: Write your name with the hand you do not normally write with. Do this three times each day. You should see an improvement in your writing after three days.

Activity 3: Hold your arm in front of you with your thumb and pointer finger about ½ inch apart. Have someone hold a yardstick between your fingers with the 0 end lined up with your finger and thumb. When they drop the stick, grab it with your finger and thumb as quickly as possible. Read the number where you grabbed the yardstick. As you practice, you should be able to grab it faster (at a lower number).

Muscles were designed to be used. As we use them, they become larger and stronger. Using muscles every day will keep them healthy. This will give you more energy and endurance for everything you do. Muscles can be torn by too much force or by a sudden force. So it is important to stretch out your muscles and start your exercise slowly so you don't tear your muscles. Take good care of your muscles so they will help you remain strong and healthy. ■

WHAT DID WE LEARN?

- What are the two types of muscles?
- How can we keep our muscles healthy?
- How do your muscles learn?
- What are some advantages of exercising?

TAKING IT FURTHER

- Do you need to exercise your facial muscles?

MUSCLE TISSUE

You learned that there are two different kinds of muscles: voluntary and involuntary. These different types of muscles are made of different types of muscle tissue. Remember how we learned that voluntary muscles have a striped appearance? The tissue that forms voluntary or skeletal muscles is called striated muscle tissue because of this striped appearance. Most muscle tissue is striated tissue.

The heart, however, is made up of special muscle tissue. The heart is composed of cardiac muscle tissue. Cardiac tissue is similar to striated tissue, except that the cardiac muscle cells are specially designed to be able to contract and relax over and over again without becoming tired. The muscles in your legs get tired fairly quickly if you are running or exercising, but cardiac muscle tissue does not get tired, even after years of constant use.

The third type of muscle tissue is smooth muscle tissue. Smooth muscle cells are very different from striated and cardiac muscle cells because they are designed for a different purpose. Smooth muscles were designed to make long, strong contractions rather than relatively short contractions. These long contractions efficiently move food through the digestive system, move blood through blood vessels, and hold your eyelids open. Each type of muscle tissue is very effective for the purposes for which it was designed.

Think about the purpose of each of the muscles listed below. Then decide if they are likely to be made of striated, cardiac, or smooth muscle tissue.

- Diaphragm
- Tongue
- Esophagus
- Mother's womb
- Hand muscle
- Heart

HANDS & FEET

Special designs from God

LESSON
10

How did God design hands and feet for their unique jobs?

Words to know:

friction skin

BEGINNERS

God designed each part of the human body for a special purpose. Two of the most amazing parts of the body are our hands and feet. God made our hands with many joints and muscles so that they would be very flexible. Hands can pick up something as small as a pin, as soft as a kitten, or as hard as brick. Hands help us to play musical instruments and scratch an itch. Hands are truly amazing. Feet are just as important. Your feet were designed to support the full weight of your body and to help you walk without falling over or tripping (at least not too often).

Look closely at the skin on your fingertips and the bottoms of your feet. What do you notice about this skin? It is different from the rest of your skin. This skin has ridges. There is a special name for this skin—**friction skin**. This special skin is what helps you to pick things up without dropping them and walk barefoot without slipping.

Finally, look at the ends of you fingers and toes. What do you see there? You have nails. These nails help protect your fingers and toes from getting hurt when you bump into things. Thank God today for your wonderful hands and feet.

• **What are some things that are special about the way that God designed your hands and feet?**

God designed each part of the human body for a special purpose. Two of the most amazing parts of the body are our hands and feet. Hands were designed for grasping, holding, and picking things up. In order to move a bite of food to your mouth, you use over 30 joints and 50 muscles. Thumbs make nearly all functions of the hand possible. The use of his hands has allowed man to accomplish the many technological, mechanical, and design marvels that we have today. Our intellect and our ability to build and manipulate things sets man apart from all of God's other creatures.

Hands have the ability to pick up something as small as a pin and as large as we can get our hands around. Your hand can hold something as delicate as a kitten and as hard as a brick. Our hands allow us to play musical instruments, type on a computer keyboard, and scratch an itch. We would be very limited in what we could

Our hands are designed to hold many different things.

DESIGN APPRECIATION

Purpose: To appreciate design of your hands and feet

Materials: a helper, pencil, cup

Procedure:

1. Try walking on your hands (get someone to help hold up your legs). How do your hands feel? Could you walk on your hands all day long?

2. Try writing your name by holding the pencil between your toes. How does this work? Why is it easier to write with your fingers than your toes?

3. Try picking up a cup without using your thumb. Now try picking it up again using your thumb and only one of your other fingers. God designed your hand with an opposing thumb—moving in the opposite direction from the fingers— to allow you to grasp objects. You can still do most things without one of your fingers but without your thumb it is almost impossible to do most activities that require grasping.

4. Try snapping your fingers without using your thumb. You can't do it. Hands and feet are perfectly designed for their functions.

Bones & Muscles

We can have fun using the hands that God gave us.

do if God did not design our hands with so much complexity. Hands have a much higher concentration of nerves and more joints than any other part of the body, which allows you to do all those fun things.

Feet were designed to support the weight of the body, and to withstand the pounding of walking, running, and jumping. Your feet can distinguish between very small changes in the surface you are walking on. Feet help us to keep our balance and to go wherever we want to go. We use our feet for hiking, swimming, and even for tickling. God made our feet tough and sensitive so we could safely navigate our world.

Both hands and feet were designed with special ridged skin called **friction skin** to help with gripping and walking. Also, fingers and toes all have nails on the ends that help protect them from injury when you bump them. ■

WHAT DID WE LEARN?

- Which is the most important finger?
- Why is the thumb so important?
- What are some special features God gave to hands and feet?

TAKING IT FURTHER

- What activities or jobs require special use of the hands?
- What jobs require special use of the feet?

ANATOMY DRAWINGS

Using an anatomy book, make detailed drawings of the bones and muscles of a hand and a foot. Label each bone and muscle in your drawings. Pay attention to the different types of joints found in each area of the foot and hand.

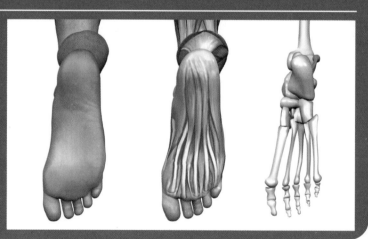

UNIT 3

NERVES & SENSES

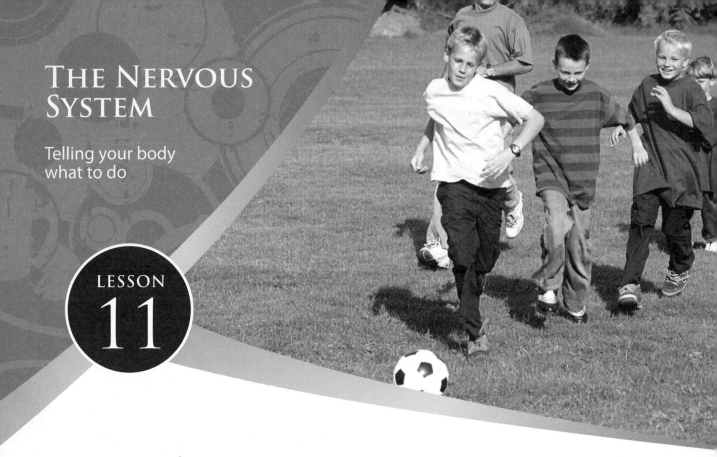

THE NERVOUS SYSTEM

Telling your body what to do

LESSON 11

How does your finger know what your brain wants it to do?

Words to know:

nervous system

central nervous system

peripheral nervous system

BEGINNERS

You have learned that your bones are moved by your muscles. You also learned that some muscles move when you think about moving them and others move without you having to think about it. Since you have to think about moving some muscles, your brain must have something to do with moving muscles.

Your brain sends special messages to your muscles to make them move. Your body has a special "highway" that carries these messages. This highway system is called your **nervous system** because it contains special cells called nerves. The highway of nerves is connected to your brain, goes down your spine, and out to all parts of your body.

The nervous system is not a one-way road. Messages travel from the brain to other parts of the body, but messages also travel from different parts of the body to the brain. This is how you feel, see, hear, taste, and smell things. We will learn more about how different parts of the nervous system work in the next several lessons.

- What is the name of the system that talks to the muscles in your body?

- What is the most important part of the nervous system?

- How do messages get from your brain to other parts of the body?

- How do messages get from your body to your brain?

Our muscular system would be useless to us without the nervous system, because our muscles would not move. The **nervous system** begins with the brain—the control center of the entire body. Connected to the brain is the spinal cord, which goes down your back. Branching off of the spinal cord is a series of nerves, which branch out to every part of the body. Together, the brain and the spinal cord are called the **central nervous system**; and the nerves, along with other organs such as the eyes and ears, are called the **peripheral nervous system**.

The nervous system has two functions. First, it sends information from the brain to the body; and second, it sends information from various parts of the body to the brain. It is a two-way information highway. When the brain is controlling the body, signals travel down the spinal cord to nerves in the muscle or other body part to be controlled. Most

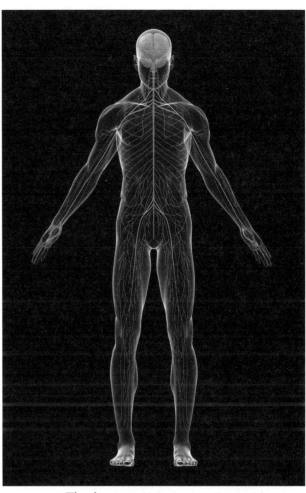

The human nervous system includes our brain, spinal cord, and many nerves throughout our body.

FUN FACT

Your funny bone is not a bone at all. It is a nerve between the bones in your elbow. When struck, it sends a message to your brain, which results in a tingly feeling in your arm and fingers.

RESPONSE TIME TEST

Purpose: To show how long it takes for a message to complete a trip from the eyes, to the brain, to the hand

Materials: small object, ruler

Procedure:

1. Place your hand flat on the table.

2. Have someone hold a small object about 3 inches above your hand and try to move your hand out of the way as they drop it.

3. Repeat this process with the object 6 inches above your hand, and then 9 inches above your hand.

Conclusion: As the object is dropped from a higher position it takes longer to fall. The time it takes to fall before you can move your hand out of the way is the time it takes for the nerve signals to make a complete trip from your eye to your brain to your arm.

NERVOUS SYSTEM COLORING PAGE

Get a copy of the "Nervous System Coloring Page" and identify and color the different parts of the nervous system. Remember that the brain and the spinal cord are the central nervous system and the collection of nerves is the peripheral nervous system.

signals are sent automatically, like ones causing your heart to beat, your lungs to breathe, and your eyes to blink. Other signals are the result of conscious thought such as signals that tell your hand to pick up a pencil or your body to lie down on the bed.

When receiving information from the body, sensory organs such as eyes, ears, or nerves in the skin send signals from the nerves up the spinal cord to the brain, where the brain processes the information and then decides what to do. Here again, many signals sent to the brain are automatic. For example, when you are running, a message saying you need more oxygen is sent to your brain from your lungs and muscles. Then your brain tells your body to increase your rate of breathing and your heart rate. Other signals occur when you purposely look at, smell, taste, listen to, or touch something. These processes will be explored more fully in later lessons. ■

WHAT DID WE LEARN?

- What are the three main parts of the nervous system?
- In the response time test, what messages were sent to and from the brain?

TAKING IT FURTHER

- Name ways that information is collected by your body to be sent to the brain.

UNIQUE HUMANS

In addition to sending and receiving signals, the human nervous system is designed to do something that no other creature can do. Humans have the ability to think, reason, and communicate with language. Humans can make decisions and show complex creativity. The human nervous system is believed by many biologists to be the most highly organized system in any living creature.

Make your own list of things that humans can do that animals cannot do. What accounts for each of these abilities?

THE BRAIN

Captain of the ship

LESSON
12

How does the brain control all of the different activities you do?

Words to know:

cerebrum

corpus callosum

cerebellum

brain stem

medulla oblongata

thalamus

pituitary gland

hippocampus

BEGINNERS

Do you know where your brain is? It is inside your head. God gave you a very strong skull to protect your brain. This is because your brain is one of the most important parts of your body. Your brain controls everything you do. It not only tells your muscles to move, but it is where you think all of your thoughts, learn and remember, see, hear, smell, and feel things.

Your brain has three parts. Two of them have big names, but you can remember them if you try. The parts of the brain are the **cerebrum** (suh-REE-bruhm), the **cerebellum** (ser-uh-BEL-uhm), and the **brain stem**. These parts of the brain control everything you do. So take good care of your brain and use it well.

• **Name some things that you do that use your brain.**

• **What are the three parts of the brain?**

The major organ of the nervous system is the brain. The brain receives, processes, and sends out billions of messages each second. It has three major parts: the cerebrum, the cerebellum, and the brain stem. The **cerebrum** (suh-REE-bruhm) is the upper part of the brain and the largest part. It controls thought, memory, and learned behavior. This is the part of the brain you use for decision making. Different areas in the cerebrum control different things. One area controls thinking, another controls speech, another memory, and so on.

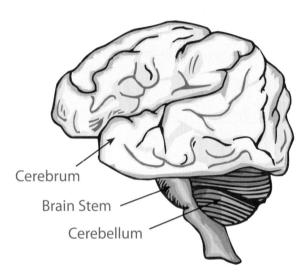

Cerebrum

Brain Stem

Cerebellum

The cerebrum is divided into two halves called the right hemisphere and the left hemisphere. The right side of the cerebrum, or right hemisphere, controls the left side of the body. It is also the "big picture" part of the brain. It helps you with artistic and geometric thoughts. It is where you appreciate humor and metaphors.

The left hemisphere controls the right side of your body and is concerned with details. You use your left hemisphere for reading, writing, arithmetic, words, and letters. The **corpus callosum** (KOR-puhs kuh-LOH-suhm)is a large mass of nerves in the center of your brain that connects the two sides.

The second major part of your brain is the **cerebellum** (ser-uh-BEL-uhm). This is the lower part of the brain. It controls balance and voluntary muscles. This part controls most of your movement. When learning a new activity, the cerebrum works with the cerebellum to think about how to do it. With practice, this function becomes more automatic and the cerebellum moves the muscles automatically. Remember when you tried to write your name with the wrong hand in lesson 9? Your cerebrum had to think very hard about how to move the muscles in that hand and arm to make your name look right. But if you practiced writing with that hand over and over, eventually your cerebellum would take over and you would not have to think about it so much, just like

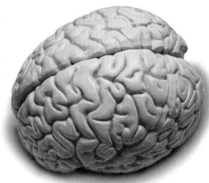

This model of a human brain shows the left and right hemispheres.

BRAIN MODEL

Using an anatomy book, make a model of the brain using different colors of clay for each of the major parts of the brain.

when you write your name with your normal writing hand.

The third major part of the brain is the **brain stem**. This is the part of the brain that connects to the spinal cord. All the messages to and from the brain pass through this part of the brain. The **medulla oblongata** (muh-DUHL-uh ob-lawng-GAH-tuh) in the brain stem is responsible for controlling involuntary muscles and regulating automatic activities, which are the necessary life functions. The brain stem regulates breathing, eye movement, heartbeat, blood pressure, waking and sleeping, and many reflexes.

Finally, several smaller parts of the brain, located near the brain stem, control other important functions. The **thalamus** (THAL-uh-muhs) routes messages to the correct part of the brain, the **pituitary gland** controls growth, and the **hippocampus** (hip-uh-KAM-puhs) helps with storage and retrieval of short-term memory. All of the parts of the brain function together to make everything else in the body work the way God designed it. This is why you need to wear your bike helmet so you don't hurt your brain if you have an accident. The brain is so complex that we can only marvel at its design, and try to copy its functions, without truly understanding it. ■

WHAT DID WE LEARN?

- What are the three major parts of the brain?
- Which part of the brain controls growth?

TAKING IT FURTHER

- Which part of the brain would be used for each of the following: running, dilating your eyes, learning your math facts?
- Is your brain the same thing as your mind?

BRAIN ANATOMY

Use an anatomy book to locate the following parts of the brain, then add them to your brain model:

- Corpus callosum
- Olfactory lobe
- Medulla oblongata
- Optic nerve
- Pituitary gland

Label the various parts of your model. You can make little flags of paper with the words and glue the papers to toothpicks. Stick these flags into your model.

For even more fun, see if you can find out in which part of the brain each of the following functions takes place:

- Thought
- Smell
- Heartbeat regulation
- Memory
- Eyesight
- Speech
- Muscle control
- Pupil dilation

LEARNING & THINKING

How do you use your brain?

LESSON 13

How do you exercise your brain?

Words to know:

cerebral cortex

BEGINNERS

Have you ever seen an animal that could read a book and understand it? Can a monkey build a building? A parrot can repeat words, but can it carry on a conversation? No. Why not? Animals' brains were not created to learn and think in the same way that human brains can. Of all of God's creatures, only man was given a mind able to think and reason at a high level.

You learned in the last lesson that your brain has different parts. Thinking happens in the part of the brain called the cerebrum. And different kinds of thinking happen in different parts of your cerebrum. You use one part of your cerebrum for reading and another part for learning your math facts.

You also learned that when you exercise it makes your muscles get stronger. The same is true for your brain. When you use your brain it gets stronger. The more you do things like reading and practicing your math facts, the easier it becomes. Then you can go on and learn even more things. Be glad that God gave you a special brain and exercise it every day.

- Are there any animals that can think and reason like people do?

- What part of your brain is used for thinking?

- How can you make your brain stronger?

The human brain is so complex we can never hope to fully understand it. God has designed our brains to not only control our bodies and to react to the world around us, but to learn and think so we can understand and enjoy the world God has created. Thinking and learning take place in the frontal lobe of the cerebrum. Also, personality, judgment, and self-control are coordinated from this part of the brain. And just as exercising your muscles makes them stronger, so exercising your brain makes it stronger.

The brain quickly learns to do things in the most efficient way so we need to constantly be challenging our brains with new ideas and tasks. We learn in many different ways. We learn by putting in new information using our five senses of sight, sound, touch, taste, and smell. These senses each connect to different parts of the cerebrum.

The hippocampus, located near the brain stem, stores and retrieves items for short-term memory. Long-term memories are stored and

FUN FACT

In 2003, a man who was barely conscious for nearly 20 years regained speech and movement because his brain spontaneously rewired itself. Doctors discovered that his brain had grown tiny new nerve connections to replace the ones sheared apart in a car crash.

BRAIN EXERCISES

Purpose: To appreciate how each side of the brain processes information differently

Materials: six index cards, colored markers

Activity 1—Procedure:

1. Take six index cards. On each index card, use a colored marker to write the name of a color. But do not write the color of the ink. For example, use the blue marker to write the word ORANGE, the orange marker to write the word GREEN, the green marker to write the word RED.

2. Now lay the index cards on the table and read the words out loud. This should be relatively easy.

3. Next, look at the word but say the color of the ink not the word that is written on the card. This will probably be much more difficult.

Conclusion: Our brains have been trained to read words regardless of the color of ink. This uses the left side of our brains. Recognizing and saying the color uses pathways to the right side that are not as strong as the verbal pathways.

Activity 2—Procedure:

Look at the pictures to the right. What do you see? Our brains are trained to interpret what we see based on what we are familiar with. In the bottom picture, do you see a duck or a rabbit? In the top picture, do you see a vase or two people facing each other?

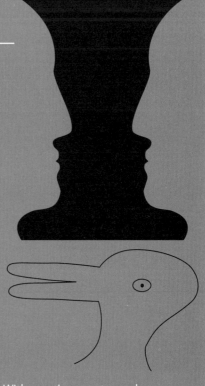

With practice, most people can see both images, but without concentration, a person usually sees only one image at first glance.

The left side of your brain is more dominant for math and logical thinking.

retrieved from the cerebral cortex, the outermost layer of the cerebrum. Most people will remember something better if it has a meaning than if it is just a picture or a sound. You can remember words or math facts better than the face of a stranger you saw only once. Also, learning something more than once greatly increases your ability to remember it. This is why you may study the human body in elementary school and then learn human anatomy again in high school.

Since different sides of the brain control different thinking skills, we need to exercise both sides of the brain. One side of the brain may be dominant or stronger than the other. People who have a stronger right side tend to be better at seeing the big picture, coming up with creative ideas, and using their intuition to solve problems. People who are left-brain dominant are good at paying attention to details, following directions, and using formal logic. But regardless of your strengths and weaknesses, you can improve in all areas of thinking with practice. So, be sure to exercise your brain every day. ■

WHAT DID WE LEARN?

- Which part of the brain does each of the following: stores short-term memories, stores long-term memories, controls learning and thinking, controls the senses?

- Which side of the brain controls the left side of the body?

- What is necessary for a healthy brain?

TAKING IT FURTHER

- List ways you can learn something.

- What is something you have trouble learning?

LOGIC PUZZLES

Try these logic puzzles to exercise your cerebrum:

1. Four people must cross a river in a boat. Two people weigh 50 pounds each and the other two weigh 100 pounds each. They have a boat that can only hold a maximum of 100 pounds without sinking. Describe how all four people can cross the river in the boat.

2. You are in a strange land and you need to find the nearest town. You know that one group of people living in the area always tells the truth and that the second group of people always tells a lie. You come to a fork in the road and do not know which way to go. Standing at the fork are two people, one from each group, but you cannot tell which one is from which group. You can only ask one person one question. What question will you ask to be sure you take the correct road to reach the nearest town?

Now that you have done a few logic puzzles, see if you can make up a logic puzzle of your own. There are many games available today that require logical thinking skills. Try to find one and play it. It will improve your brain power.

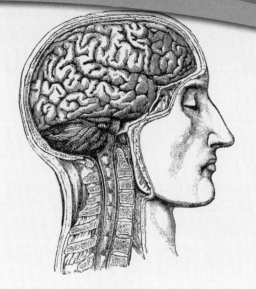

Brain Surgery

The brain is very complex and still far more powerful than the most advanced computers. Very little was known about the human brain until the last 100 years or so. However, this did not stop man from conducting brain surgery. "Trepanning," the process of putting a small hole 1 to 2 inches (2.5–5 cm) in diameter into the skull of a living patient, goes back to ancient times. Records and bones show that this procedure was practiced in Ancient Egypt, as well as in Greece and Rome. Records show that the operation has also been done in the Middle East, in China, among the Celtic tribes, in India, among the Mayans, Aztecs, and the Brazilian Indians, in the South Seas, and in Africa.

If so little was known about the brain, why was there such widespread trepanning? No one really knows. The surprising part of all this is that the survival rate among patients that had this procedure may have been as high as 65 to 70% in ancient times. This is a much higher survival rate than what brain surgery patients experienced in the 14th through the 18th centuries. Did the ancient people have knowledge about the brain from before the Flood that was later lost? We may never know.

During the Middle Ages, no real advancement was made in understanding the brain. Then in the 1800s, Eduard Hitzig, a German doctor working at a military hospital, conducted some experiments. His patients had suffered head injuries on the battlefield, leaving part of the skull missing. Using a battery, he stimulated the back area of their brains. He found that by doing so he was able to make their eyes move.

Later, he teamed up with Gustav Fritsch and ran experiments on dogs. They found, through stimulating the dogs' brains, that specific areas of the brain controlled specific movements.

Later, John Jackson learned more by observing epileptic seizures in his wife. He found that the seizures always followed the same pattern. He believed that electrical pulses starting in one part of the brain and radiating out to other parts caused the seizures. From these observations he determined that the brain was divided into different sections, each controlling a different motor function.

Scientists discovered that the brain also affects personality when a man named Phineas Gage was injured in 1848. While working as a railroad construction supervisor, an explosion accidentally sent a rod through the left side of his skull. The rod, about an inch in diameter, entered though his left cheek and exited through the top of his head. He recovered from the injury, but months later started showing startling changes in his personality. He became anti-social, foul-mouthed and a liar, which was very unlike his original personality. This was believed to be a result of his injury.

These 19th-century discoveries were the beginning of understanding the brain. Today, scientists have a better understanding of the brain. They know how electrical signals travel throughout the nervous system. They know which regions in the brain control thought and movement. Doctors can "look" at a person's brain without opening the skull using CAT scans (computerized axial tomography) and MRI (magnetic resonance imaging).

Using modern technology, surgeons today can do many types of operations that greatly benefit the patient without causing damage to the brain. Brain surgery today has a 98% success rate. Technology allows surgeons to make smaller incisions compared to surgery in the past. Also, microscopic cameras allow the surgeons to see exactly what they are doing so they only touch the necessary parts of the brain. Brain surgery has come a long way from the trepanning of ancient times.

But even with all of their knowledge, people still don't really understand how the brain helps us think, feel, and make decisions. God, in His infinite wisdom, has created our brains with a complexity that we will never fully understand.

REFLEXES & NERVES

Faster than lightning

How do electrical signals travel through your body?

Words to know:

reflex

neuron

Challenge words:

sensory neurons

motor neurons

interneurons

association neurons

dendrite

axon

Schwann cells

myelin

BEGINNERS

Close your eyes and have another person hand you something. Keep your eyes closed and try to describe the item. How does it feel? What is its shape? Can you tell what it is? How were you able to tell what it was?

You could tell something about the item because you could feel the shape, size, and texture of the object. The reason you can feel these things is because your skin contains nerves. Nerves are cells that are specially designed to take messages to and from the brain. When you touch something, the nerves in your hand feel it and tell your brain about it. Then your brain sends a message to your hand to move or to pick up the item. These nerves help you pick up a pencil or pet a soft puppy.

If you touch something that is very hot, you need to move your hand away very quickly. You don't have time for a message to get all the way to your brain and back to your hand before you get burned. God designed your body with the ability to move very quickly when you are in danger. This very quick movement is called a **reflex**. The message for a reflex only travels to your spine instead of to your brain so it is faster. Another reflex is when you close your eyes if you think something is flying toward them. God made your body to be able to be safe in this sin-cursed world.

• **What is in your skin that helps you feel things?**

• **What allows you to move very quickly when you are in danger?**

Some functions of your nervous system are automatic—you don't have to think about them. One automatic function is called a **reflex**. A reflex is when your body moves quickly in response to something. For example, if something flies toward your face, you automatically close your eyes. If you set your hand on something hot, you quickly jerk it back. God designed us to have reflexes so we would be less likely to get hurt.

Reflexes occur when a danger signal, such as "it's hot," is sent to the spinal cord and another message is sent directly to the hand to make it move, without the message having to go all the way to the brain. This path is shorter so it is quicker, allowing us to react more quickly to a dangerous situation. If we are not in danger, messages generally go all the way to the brain to be processed.

Whether the message goes all the way to the brain or just to the spinal cord, nerves receive the information from outside the body. All of our senses contain nerves. There are special nerves in the eyes, ears, nose, and tongue, but most nerves that receive information are on the surface of our skin. Nerve cells called **neurons** send pulses of electricity to the brain.

We have nerves all over our bodies, but they are more concentrated in our hands, feet, and face than in other parts of our bodies. More nerves are needed in our fingers to enable us to detect subtle differences in the things we touch. There are several

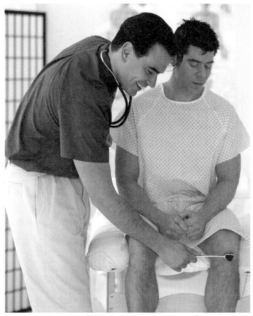
Doctors often check our reflexes.

TEST YOUR REFLEXES & NERVES

To test your reflexes, a doctor may have hit your knee lightly with a rubber hammer. Were you surprised to see your leg jump? You can do the same thing at home.

Purpose: To test your own reflexes

Materials: toothpicks or pencils, blindfold

Activity 1—Procedure:

Sit with one leg crossed over the other and have someone gently strike your leg just below the kneecap with the side of his hand. If you are relaxed, you should see your leg kick out even though you didn't mean for it to.

Activity 2—Procedure:

1. Have someone blindfold you or sit in such a way that you cannot see what they are doing.

2. Have them gently press the two points of the pencils against your finger tip with the tips touching each other. How many points do you feel? You should only feel one point.

3. Lift and repeat with the tips slightly apart.

4. Repeat, spreading the points farther apart until you can feel two distinct points. Measure

how far apart the tips were when you felt two points.

5. Now repeat this exercise on the back of your arm. The points should be much farther apart before you can distinguish two separate points.

Conclusion: You can repeat this exercise on various parts of your body such as the bottoms of your feet or your back. You should discover that nerves are much closer together on the fingers and feet than other places.

different types of nerves in the skin. These different nerves detect different sensations. Some nerves detect touch/texture, pain, or temperature. Others detect vibration and rapid pressure changes. Still others detect slight pressure changes. All of these nerves work together to help us interpret the world around us. ■

WHAT DID WE LEARN?

- How do reflex reactions differ from other nervous system messages?
- Why do we have reflexes?
- What are some different types of sensations detected by your nerves?

TAKING IT FURTHER

- What reflexes might you experience?
- How does the sense of touch differ from your fingertips to the back of your arm?
- Why do you need a larger number of nerves on the bottoms of your feet?

NERVE CELLS

God designed your body with millions of nerves, also called neurons, to help you do all the things you need to do. These nerve cells are divided into three different categories. First, you have sensory neurons. Sensory neurons receive information from outside the body and send messages to the brain. The nerves in your skin are sensory nerves. You also have sensory nerves in your mouth for taste and in your nose for smell. The optic nerves in your eyes and the auditory nerves in your ears are sensory nerves as well.

The second type of nerves is motor neurons. Motor neurons transfer electrical impulses from the brain to your muscles. These are the nerves that make your arms and legs move. They also carry messages to your heart to make it keep beating and to your diaphragm to make you keep breathing.

Finally, you have interneurons, also called association neurons. Interneurons are the nerves in your brain and spinal cord that receive

and interpret the information from the sensory nerves and then pass instructions to the motor nerves. These nerves work somewhat like the logic circuits in a computer.

Nerve cells have a nucleus that controls the metabolism of the cell. The nucleus is located in the cell body. Connected to the cell body are hundreds or even thousands of tiny fingers called dendrites. Dendrites receive input. This input can come from outside your body or from another nerve cell. The electrical impulse received by the dendrite is then passed on to the cell body which in turn passes it on to the axon. The axon is a long projection that carries the impulse away from the cell body to another neuron. The axon is covered by special cells called Schwann cells which produce a material called myelin. Myelin acts as insulation, preventing electrical signals from jumping between nerve cells. The electrical signals in your nervous system always

travel from the dendrites toward the axons. Dendrites are usually relatively short, but axons can be very long, sometimes as long as one yard (one meter).

Draw a diagram of a nerve cell and label all of the parts. Do some research on multiple sclerosis, a disease of the nervous system. Find out what causes it and how it affects the nerves.

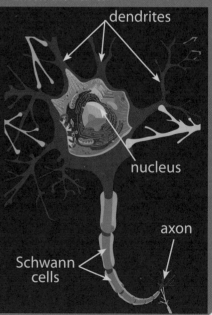

dendrites

nucleus

Schwann cells

axon

THE FIVE SENSES

Letting your brain know what's out there

How many different ways can you sense an orange?

Challenge words:

Braille

BEGINNERS

There are five ways that your body tells your brain what is going on around you. Can you name any of them? You can see, hear, smell, taste, and touch things. These are called your five senses. Remember when you tried to describe an object with your eyes closed? You had to use your sense of touch. What were some things you could tell about the object just by touching it? You could tell how big it was, whether it was soft or hard, and its general shape. What were some things you could not tell just by touching it? You could not tell what color it was, or if it had any pictures or patterns on it. You must use your sense of sight to tell these things.

God designed each of your senses to tell you something different about the world around you. Your body works best when you use all five senses together to get information. Some people may not be able to see or hear. Then the other senses help to provide some information. If a person cannot see, they can often hear things that a seeing person might not hear.

Which part of your body do you use for sight? Your eyes. Which part do you use for hearing? Your ears. Which part of your body helps you taste things? Your tongue. Which part helps you smell things? Your nose. Which part of your body helps you touch and feel things?

You might say your hands or fingers and you are right. But, you actually can feel things with every part of your skin. Only a few parts of your body do not have nerves so you cannot feel anything there. These parts are your hair, your fingernails, and your toenails.

- **What are your five senses?**

- **What are the parts of your body that provide these senses?**

- **What parts of your body cannot feel anything?**

We input information to our nervous system through our five senses: touch, taste, smell, sight, and hearing. Most people use all five senses together in various degrees throughout the day. We get the most information through our sense of sight. But if one sense is not working properly, the other senses can help compensate.

Blind people read using the Braille alphabet of raised dots.

A blind person has heightened hearing and touch to help make up for not seeing. The use of touch can help a blind person read using the Braille alphabet of raised dots. Similarly, a deaf person has a heightened sense of sight and touch. A deaf person can often feel something that a hearing person could not.

In addition to collecting information about the world around us, our senses tell us things about our own bodies. Our senses tell us where the parts of our body are in relation to things around us. Receptors in muscles and joints send messages to the brain so it knows where our body parts are. Our senses also help us keep our balance. Receptors in the inner ear help tell us when we are off balance.

We often associate the sense of touch with our fingers or hands. But actually, this sense occurs throughout your entire body. As we discussed in the previous lesson, more nerves are located in the hands and feet, but there are nerves that touch the world around you everywhere you have skin. These nerves can sometimes cause curious results. Have you ever wondered what causes goose bumps? Nerves attached to the hairs on your skin detect breezes or cold temperatures and your brain causes small muscles attached to the hair follicles to contract. This movement causes goose bumps and helps to warm you up. It also alerts your brain to have you take more action if necessary to warm you up.

A few parts of your body do not have nerves. Your hair, fingernails, and toenails do not have nerves. This is

FUN FACT

The nerves throughout your body can send pain messages to the brain. Medicines can help relieve pain, but the brain can also produce its own pain relievers called endorphins. Soothing music can also help your brain block pain messages so you don't feel so uncomfortable.

FEELING HOT, FEELING COLD

Nerves in your skin can distinguish many different sensations including temperature, pressure, pain, and vibration.

Purpose: To understand how our body reacts to temperature differences

Materials: 3 bowls, jacket with zipper, straight pins, bag of ice

Activity 1—Procedure:

1. Set up three bowls of water: one hot (not hot enough to burn the skin), one warm (about room temperature), and one cold.

2. Place one hand in the bowl of hot water and the other hand in the bowl of cold water for 1–2 minutes.

3. At the end of that time, immediately place both your hands in the bowl of warm water. How does the warm water feel to each hand?

4. Keep your hands in the warm water for 1–2 minutes. How does the water feel to each hand at the end of that time?

Conclusion: Over time, if the same message is sent to the brain over and over, and it is not an emergency type of signal, the brain will often start ignoring it. So your hands do not notice how hot or cold the water is. Also, the brain makes assumptions about temperature in a relative way. If something is much colder or hotter than what you have been experiencing, the brain notices it more strongly. That is why the warm water feels cold to the hand that was in the hot water and it feels hot to the hand that was in the cold water.

Activity 2—Procedure:

1. Put on a jacket with a zipper but leave it unzipped.

2. Place 2–3 straight pins on a table.

3. Hold a bag of ice in your hands for 2–3 minutes, then try to zip up the jacket.

4. Next, try to pick up the pins one at a time. This may seem difficult to do with very cold hands.

Conclusion: Extended cold signals are eventually ignored by the brain, making it slower to respond to other inputs from that hand. This makes the hand feel numb and unable to do many of the normal tasks. If an area of skin is exposed to extreme cold for long periods of time, the skin can be damaged. But if it is cold for only a short period of time, like in this experiment, the signals quickly begin flowing again and normal activity resumes.

why you can cut your hair and your nails without feeling pain. We will explore the sense of touch in today's activity, and we will learn more about the other senses in following lessons. ■

WHAT DID WE LEARN?

- What are your five senses?
- Which of these senses usually gives us the most information?
- How does your brain compensate for the loss of one of your senses?

TAKING IT FURTHER

- You have nerves all over your skin, so why don't you feel your clothes all day long?
- Your eyes see your nose all day long. Why don't you notice it all the time?
- If you are in the hot sun for a while then you go inside, the room feels cold. Why?

BRAILLE SYSTEM

Because people without the sense of sight still need a form of written communication, Louis Braille developed a special alphabet for blind people. His alphabet is a system of raised dots that represent letters and numbers. The Braille system starts with a matrix of six dots in two columns with three dots in each. The location of the raised dots in this matrix determines the letter. For example if there is a dot in the upper left hand position only, this represents the letter *a*. If there is a dot in the two upper positions only, this represents the letter *c*. Below is a chart showing all of the letters of the Braille alphabet.

The same patterns are used to represent some of the numerals as are used for some of the letters, so a special pattern precedes numbers to notify the reader that what follows is a number.

There are machines that are designed to print books and other papers using the Braille alphabet. Blind people can use these machines to write letters and to have written communication with other people.

Write a message on a piece of paper in Braille using small dots of glue for the raised dots. Allow the glue to dry, then try to read the message with your fingers. Allow a schoolmate or family member to try to read your Braille message as well. Why do you think that Braille was designed to be read with fingertips instead of your palm or the side of your hand?

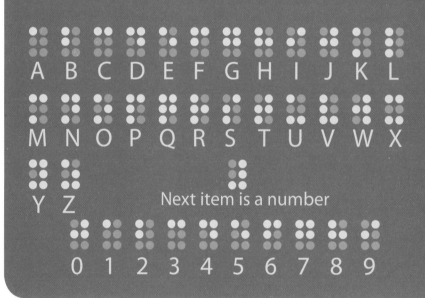

Louis Braille

THE EYE

Window to the world

LESSON 16

BEGINNERS

Look at your eye in the mirror. Describe what you see. You should see a dark circle in the middle of your eye. This is called the **pupil**. The pupil lets light into your eye. Around your pupil is a colored circle. This is called the iris. The **iris** contains muscles that make your pupil get bigger or smaller depending on how much light is in the room. You should also see eyelids and eyelashes. These protect your eyes from dirt and other things that might get into them.

God designed this amazing body part to allow you to see the world around you. Light bounces off of objects around you. This light enters your eye and forms a picture inside your eye. This picture is sent along the **optic nerve** to your brain where you then see the picture. The eye is a truly amazing organ.

- What are some parts of your eye that you can see when you look in the mirror?
- What is the purpose of the pupil?
- What is the purpose of the iris?
- What carries the picture from your eye to your brain?

One of the most complex and useful of our five senses is sight. The organ for sight is the eye. The eye receives light rays that bounce off of objects around us. The light passes through the **cornea**, the front of the eye, and enters the **pupil**, which is the dark circle in the middle of your eye. It then passes through the **lens**, which focuses and projects an upside down image on the **retina**, which is the back of the eye. Receptors in the retina called **rods** and **cones** detect light and color and change the image into electrical signals that are sent to the **optic nerve**, which sends the message on to the brain. The brain interprets the signal, turns the image right side up, and lets you see the object. All of this happens in a fraction of a second.

Your brain controls the parts of your eye to help you see most efficiently. The brain causes muscles in the **iris**, the colored part surrounding your pupil, to widen or narrow the pupil to allow in the best amount of light. In a dark room your pupils get very wide to enable you to use all available light. In very bright light the pupils get very small to protect the eye and optic nerve from overload. The brain also changes the shape of the lens to keep objects in focus. This allows you to look at objects that are very near as well as at things that are far away. The brain also controls the muscles that move the eyes to keep them working together.

Your brain and eyes work together to help you recognize things you are familiar with. You use four kinds of

Fun Fact

It's estimated that up to 8% of boys have some degree of color blindness, whereas less than 1% of girls have the same condition.

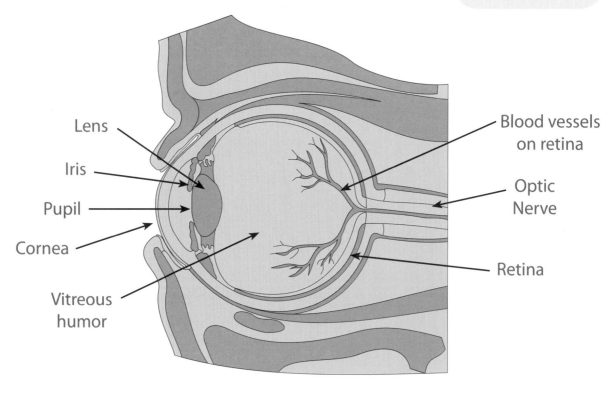

Lens

Iris

Pupil

Cornea

Vitreous humor

Blood vessels on retina

Optic Nerve

Retina

FOOLING YOUR EYES

Purpose: To better understand how your eyes work

Materials: paper tube, piece of paper, pencil, marker

Activity 1—Procedure:

1. Hold a paper tube to one eye and place your other hand beside the tube with the palm facing you.

2. While looking straight ahead with both eyes, slowly move the hand closer or farther away from your face.

Conclusion: You should be able to see a "hole" through your hand. This is because each eye sees a different image. Your brain takes the images from both eyes and combines them into one image.

Activity 2—Procedure:

1. Hold your arm straight out with one finger sticking up.

2. Close one eye and focus on something on the wall across the room.

3. Alternate which eye you have open and which you have closed.

Conclusion: You should see your finger "jump" back and forth with respect to whatever you are focusing on. The finger appears to move even though it is stationary because each eye views the finger and the wall from a different position. This blending of images from different perspectives is what allows you to have depth perception.

Activity 3—Procedure:

1. Take a 3-inch by 6-inch piece of paper and draw a small star ½ inch from the left edge and draw a small circle ½ inch from the right edge. Color in both shapes so they are easy to see.

2. Hold the paper at arm's length and close your left eye.

3. While looking at the star with your right eye, slowly bring the paper closer to your face. Notice at what point the circle disappears.

4. Repeat by using your left eye to look at the circle and see where the star disappears.

Conclusion: The shape disappears because your eye has a blind spot where the optic nerve attaches to the back of the eyeball. Your brain fills in the blanks from what it sees around the blind spot. At a certain point the brain only sees the blank paper and cannot fill in the circle or star. As you bring the paper closer or farther away, your eye can detect enough of the image for your brain to fill in the rest.

Activity 4—Procedure:

1. Look at the image below. What figure do you see in the center?

2. If you looked from left to right you probably thought it was a B, but if you read it from top to bottom you probably saw a 13. Your brain associates images with those around it to determine what you are seeing.

12
A 13 C
14

"clues" to help you determine what something is: shape, size, brightness, and color. A favorite toy can be recognized hiding under a bed by its size and shape even if you can't see it very well. If you don't have enough light, or you can't see all of something, your brain automatically fills in the gaps and tries to match it to something you know. This can result in your eyes being fooled into seeing something they don't really see. Illusionists use this knowledge to trick their audiences all the time. ■

WHAT DID WE LEARN?

- Name four important parts of the eye.
- How does your brain compensate for different amounts of light in your surroundings?
- How does your brain help you to focus on items that are near and items that are far away?
- Why did God design our bodies with two eyes instead of just one?
- How does having two eyes help with a 3-dimensional image?
- Since you have a blind spot, how can you see what is in that spot?

TAKING IT FURTHER

- Name some ways that the eye is protected from harm.
- Why do some people have to wear glasses or contact lenses?
- Why can you fool your eyes or your brain into thinking you saw something you didn't actually see?

LIQUID IN YOUR EYES

In order to work properly, your eyeball must maintain its general size and shape. Your eyes have two different liquids that help it to do this. First, the aqueous humor is a liquid between the cornea and the lens. This liquid keeps the front of the eye firm. It also serves the function of blood by providing nutrients to the front of the eyeball. However, unlike blood, the aqueous humor is clear so it does not interfere with the light passing through the eye.

The second liquid is in the center of the eyeball. This liquid is called the vitreous humor. It is a clear jelly-like substance that helps to keep the eyeball firm.

Using an anatomy book, draw a detailed diagram of the eye. Be sure to label each of the following parts of the eye. Below your drawing, briefly describe the function of each part.

- Lens
- Pupil
- Iris
- Cornea
- Rods
- Cones
- Retina
- Optic Nerve
- Vitreous humor
- Aqueous humor

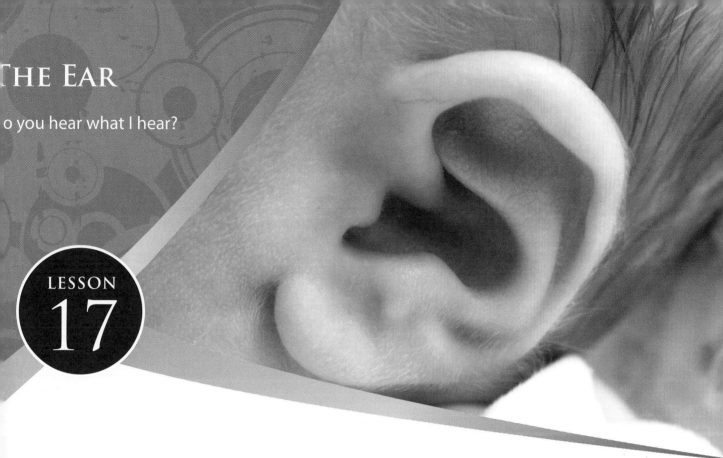

THE EAR

o you hear what I hear?

low does the ear
detect sound?

ords to know:

uditory canal

ochlea

equency

mplitude

allenge words:

ustachian tube

emicircular canals

BEGINNERS

Close your eyes. Try to identify as many different sounds around you as you can. Do you hear someone talking? Do you hear your own breathing? Do you hear birds outside? Do you hear the refrigerator running in the kitchen? We tend to ignore many sounds around us, but God designed our ears to hear even small sounds.

When you think about your ears, what do you think of? You probably think about the ears on the sides of your head. But this is only part of what allows you to hear all the sounds around you. There are many parts of the ear inside your head that allow sound to be transferred to your brain where you actually hear it.

The sound enters your outer ear and pushes against your eardrum. This causes three tiny bones inside your ear to move. The movement of these bones makes the sound move to the auditory nerve, which carries the sound to your brain. Look at the diagram on the next page to see where all of these parts are inside your ear.

Some people cannot hear. If you cannot hear it is very difficult to learn to speak. But, these people can still talk to other people using a special language called sign language. People using sign language make special signs with their hands to say words. So even if you cannot hear, you can speak to other people.

- **Name three parts of your ear that are inside your head.**

- **How do people who cannot hear speak with other people?**

What is a sound and how do you hear it? Sounds are vibrations of the air that travel in waves. These waves of vibrating air enter your ear through the opening of the ear, called the auditory canal, and hit your eardrum, causing it to vibrate. Those vibrations are passed on through three tiny bones in your middle ear, called the malleus, incus, and stapes, to the cochlea, which is a snail-shaped tube filled with liquid. The waves are then converted into electrical impulses and sent by the auditory nerve to the brain. The brain then interprets these signals as sounds.

Sound waves have two parts: frequency (pitch) and amplitude (loudness). The closer together the waves are, the higher the pitch. The peaks of a sound wave from a whistle would be much closer together than those from a bass drum. The bigger the waves are, the louder the sound. Sound waves from a loud sound are very tall, whereas a whisper produces very short waves. The differences in waves allow us to hear a large variety of sounds. Most sounds that we hear are not just one pitch but are some combination of pitches.

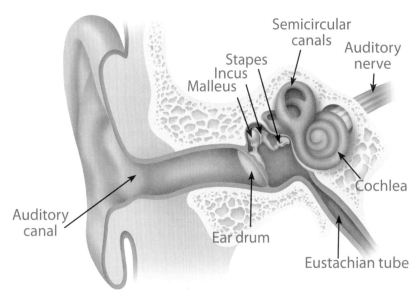

Semicircular canals
Auditory nerve
Stapes
Incus
Malleus
Auditory canal
Ear drum
Cochlea
Eustachian tube

Some people have difficulty hearing or cannot hear at all. These people must learn to communicate differently than hearing people. Many deaf people communicate using sign language. Many also learn to read lips by watching the speaker's lips, tongue, and throat muscles. Generally, lip readers can read about half of the words and must guess at the rest.

Some people are born deaf; others have diseases that destroy their hearing. But many people become partially or completely deaf by being exposed to very loud

HEARING WORKSHEET

Complete the "Do You Hear What I Hear?" worksheet.

Loudness is measured in decibels. The quieter the sound, the lower the decibels. Falling snow is so quiet it has a loudness of 0 decibels (dB). A jet engine is so loud it is about 140 dB. Most people watch TV at a level of about 70dB, but a whisper is much quieter.

noises. We can protect our hearing by wearing earplugs or other ear protectors when we must be around loud noises. We can also try to avoid loud noises that might damage our ears. God has given us wonderful senses to interact with our world, and we must take care of them. ■

WHAT DID WE LEARN?

- What determines how high or low a sound will be?
- What determines how loud or soft a sound will be?

TAKING IT FURTHER

- Why do two different instruments playing the same note at the same loudness sound different?
- Name several ways to protect your hearing.
- How do you suppose deaf children learn to speak?
- How do you think a CD player or a telephone makes sounds?

EAR ANATOMY

The ear is divided into three areas. The outer ear is the stiff part on the side of your head. The outer ear is made of cartilage, which gives it its shape and stiffness. The purpose of the outer ear is to catch and direct sound waves down the auditory canal to the ear drum. Although the auditory canal is inside the head it is usually classified as part of the outer ear.

From the eardrum to the cochlea is considered the middle ear. The middle ear contains the three bones mentioned earlier in the lesson as well as the eustachian tube. The eustachian tube is a tube that goes from the ear to the throat. This tube helps regulate the pressure on your eardrum and middle ear. If you have ever been on an airplane or driving in the

mountains you have probably experienced the urge to yawn and then had your ears "pop." This occurs because the pressure outside your ear was different than the pressure inside your ear. By yawning, you opened up the eustachian tubes allowing the pressure to equalize. The purpose of the middle ear is to move the sound waves from air to liquid.

Your inner ear contains the cochlea where sound vibrations are converted to electrical impulses and sent by the auditory nerve to the brain. The inner ear also contains what are called the semicircular canals. These canals are three tiny tubes filled with liquid. The liquid in these tubes indicate to your brain what direction you are moving. One

tube detects forward and backward movement. One detects up and down movement. The third detects movement right or left. These tubes are responsible for helping you keep your balance.

Close your eyes and stand in one place. Were you able to do it? You probably had very little trouble keeping upright even with your eyes closed because your inner ear helps you keep your balance. Now, with your eyes closed, have someone spin you around several times. Keep your eyes closed and try to stand in one place. You probably had trouble doing this. This is because the liquid in your inner ear keeps moving even after your body stops so your brain is confused for a few moments about where your body is.

TASTE & SMELL

What's for dinner?

LESSON 18

How many different things can you taste?

Challenge words:

papillae

gustatory receptor cells

olfactory hairs

odorant

BEGINNERS

Imagine your favorite food. What does it taste like? You can taste four basic tastes: sweet, salty, sour, and bitter. What foods do you usually think of as sweet? Candy, ice cream, and cookies are sweet foods. What foods do you think are salty? Chips and popcorn usually have salt added to them so they taste salty. What foods are sour? A lemon is very sour, that is why sugar is added to lemon juice to make lemonade. And what foods are bitter? We usually don't like bitter foods unless they have sugar added, too. Chocolate has a very bitter flavor but tastes good when sugar is added to it. Most foods are a combination of sweet, salty, sour, and bitter.

Think about how your favorite food smells. Your sense of taste and smell work together to help you enjoy the food that you eat. If you cannot smell the food, it does not taste as good. So enjoy the tastes and smells of the things God has given you to eat.

- **What are the four basic flavors?**
- **What sense works together with taste to give you the full flavor of food?**

Your tongue and your nose work together to help you decide which foods are safe and good to eat. Things that are bad for you generally taste pretty bad, though not always. Most things that are good for you are pleasant to taste, although those of you who dislike vegetables may not agree. Your tongue determines taste and your nose determines smell. However, one without the other does not give you the full flavor of the food.

You taste various flavors with your taste buds. A taste bud is a bump surrounded by a trench that traps saliva. The taste receptors in the trenches convert tastes into electrical signals that go to the brain. Most tastes buds are located on the surface of your tongue, but you also have some taste buds on the roof of your mouth and even a few in your throat. If you look closely in a mirror, you can see the taste buds on your tongue.

Your taste buds can detect four basic tastes: sweet, salty, sour, and bitter. Some scientists include a fifth taste called umami. This is a flavor that is common in Asian foods, and is found in a chemical call MSG.

However, a combination of these four or five tastes cannot account for the wide range of flavors we experience. The nose has smell receptors inside the nasal cavity that send signals to the brain at the same time the taste buds are sending taste signals. The brain uses all this information to allow you to taste the food. This is why sometimes when you smell something, like chocolate chip cookies in the oven, you can almost taste them, too.

Map of the Tongue

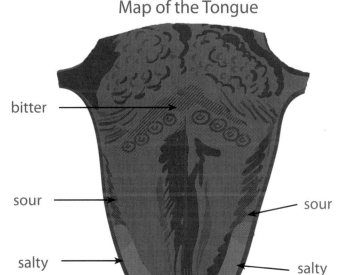

bitter

sour — — sour

salty — — salty

— sweet

TASTE WITHOUT SALIVA?

Purpose: To determine whether saliva is necessary for taste

Materials: Paper towels, salt, sugar

Procedure:

1. Dry your tongue with a paper towel to remove as much saliva as possible.

2. Sprinkle a small amount of salt on your tongue. Can you taste the salt? You won't be able to taste it if your tongue is dry, because the salt must be dissolved in saliva before your taste buds can detect it.

3. Rinse your tongue off with water.

4. Repeat steps 1–3 with sugar instead of salt. Again, you won't be able to taste the sugar if your tongue is dry.

SMELL DETECTIVE

Collect several items with distinctive odors. Close your eyes and have someone hold each item for you to sniff. How many you can identify just by smell?

TASTE WITHOUT SMELL

Peel a potato, apple, and carrot and cut each into the same size cubes. Close your eyes and plug your nose and then have someone feed you one cube of each item. How difficult was it to tell the difference between the foods without using your nose? Repeat this activity without plugging your nose. Was it easier for you to tell which food was which? It should be.

FUN FACT

You have almost 10,000 taste buds inside your mouth— even some on the roof of your mouth.

Scientists used to think there were only four basic smells: fragrant, fresh, spicy, and putrid. Other scientists have classified smells into seven categories: minty, floral, ethereal, musky, resinous, foul, and acrid. More recent studies have revealed that there may be hundreds or even thousands of smells. This is an area in which more research is being done.

The tongue responds to chemicals dissolved in saliva. The nose responds to chemicals in the air. Together, these chemical messages are changed into electronic messages that are interpreted by the brain. This allows you to enjoy your meal, sometimes even your veggies. ■

FUN FACT

Smells are often linked to memories— sometimes pleasant and sometimes unpleasant. When you smell a particular scent again a memory comes back to you. Can you describe a time when a smell triggered a memory?

WHAT DID WE LEARN?

- What four flavors can your tongue detect?
- How does your tongue detect flavors?
- How does your nose detect fragrances?

TAKING IT FURTHER

- Can you still taste foods when you have a stuffy nose?
- Smells are used for more things than just enjoying food. List some other uses for your sense of smell.
- Oranges and grapefruits are both sweet and sour. Why do they taste different?
- Cocoa is very bitter. Why does chocolate candy taste so delicious?

Nerves & Senses

HOW WE TASTE AND SMELL

Let's take a closer look at how tastes and smells actually get to your brain. Taste and smell are both chemical reactions. In order to taste something the food must be dissolved in the saliva in your mouth. Your tongue is covered with taste buds called **papillae**, which are bumps with special cells that react with the chemicals in

saliva. These special cells are called **gustatory receptor cells**. As the saliva passes over the gustatory receptor cells on the papillae, a chemical reaction takes place in these cells, which sends an electrical signal to your brain so that you can taste the flavor that particular cell can detect.

A similar process takes place in your nasal cavity. When you sniff air into your nasal cavity it passes over **olfactory hairs**, which are actually extensions of the dendrites of the olfactory nerves. These hairs bond with very light molecules called **odorants**. Food, flowers, perfume, and other items with distinctive scents have odorants, which are light molecules that easily evaporate. Items that have no scent do not have molecules that easily evaporate. When the olfactory hairs bond with the odorants, a chemical

reaction takes place that then sends an electrical signal to your brain and you smell the odor.

Think about how taste and smell are different from your other senses. What is the input to each of your senses? The five senses have very different inputs, but in the end you sense something because the input has been changed into an electrical signal that goes to your brain where it is processed.

UNIT 4

DIGESTION

THE DIGESTIVE SYSTEM

What happens to my lunch?

LESSON
19

Where does digestion begin and end?

Words to know:

digestive system

enzyme

esophagus

stomach

small intestine

villi

large intestine

Challenge words:

salivary amylase

gastric juice

bile

pancreatic juice

sodium bicarbonate

BEGINNERS

Your body needs energy to move and play. You get this energy from the food you eat. The part of your body that takes the energy out of the food is your **digestive system**.

When you eat your food, your teeth break it into small pieces. When you swallow, these small pieces go into your **stomach** where chemicals help break the food into very tiny pieces. After the food has spent from 30 minutes to 3 hours in your stomach it passes into your small intestine.

Your **small intestine** is a tube that absorbs the food molecules into your blood, where they are then taken to all parts of your body to give you energy. Some parts of what you eat cannot be used for energy and these parts pass out of the small intestine into the **large intestine** and then out of your body when you go to the bathroom.

You need to eat the right foods so that your body has all of the energy it needs for you to move and grow. We will learn more about the kinds of food you should eat in another lesson.

- **What system of your body gets the energy out of the food you eat?**

- **Name three parts of your digestive system.**

- **How do food molecules get to all parts of your body?**

Your body needs energy to run and jump, to skate, and to ride a bike. It also needs nutrients to build strong bones and muscles and to help you grow. God designed your digestive system to give you the nutrients and energy you need.

The **digestive system** begins in your mouth, where your tongue and teeth work together to break food into small pieces that can be easily swallowed. Saliva glands squirt saliva into your mouth. Saliva contains various **enzymes**, chemicals that help with digestion, to help begin the process of breaking down your food. The food then travels down the **esophagus**—a tube starting at the back of your throat that leads to your stomach.

In the **stomach**, water and hydrochloric acid break down the food particles and the stomach churns the food until it is a thin liquid consistency. Food spends from 30 minutes to 3 hours in your stomach, depending on what you ate. When it is broken down enough, it leaves the stomach and enters the small intestine.

The **small intestine** is a tube about 19 feet long that coils back and forth inside your body. It is lined with finger-like projections called **villi**. The food molecules pass through the villi membrane and into the blood stream where they are taken throughout the body and converted into energy. Then the nutrients are used to build up your body.

The parts of the food that cannot be used are passed on into the large intestine. This is a tube that is wider but shorter than the small intestine. In the **large intestine** water is removed and the unusable parts of the food pass out of the body.

All of the parts of the digestive system work together to effi-

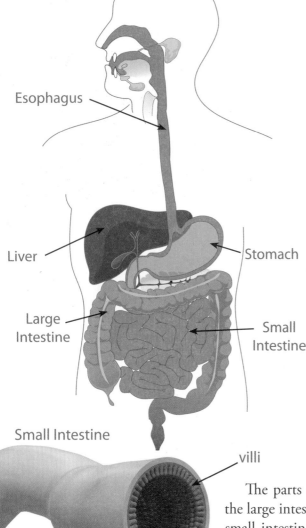

Esophagus

Liver

Large Intestine

Stomach

Small Intestine

Small Intestine

villi

Digestion

WHERE'S MY LUNCH?

Fill out the "Where's My Lunch?" worksheet while you begin to eat a sandwich for lunch. Mark down the time you begin eating your sandwich, the time you complete eating it, and the times that you expect the sandwich to reach each part of your digestive system. Place the worksheet in a visible place and check it periodically throughout the next 2–3 days to find the approximate location of your sandwich.

ciently absorb the usable parts of the food and expel what cannot be used. Digestion is partly a mechanical process, with the teeth grinding the food, but it is mostly a chemical process. Chemicals are added to your food in your mouth, stomach, and intestines. These chemicals aid in breaking down the food into its basic nutrients.

There are several things you can do to keep your digestive system healthy. First, you need to eat the right foods. Eating a balanced diet helps keep your entire body working efficiently and helps you feel better. You need to eat foods from all the food groups including foods with fiber. Also, you need to drink enough liquids to ensure proper digestion. Exercise is also important to keeping your digestive system functioning properly. Finally, try and avoid negative feelings such as fear or anxiety near mealtimes. These can cause you to experience stomachaches and headaches. ■

WHAT DID WE LEARN?

- What are the main parts of the digestive system?
- What role do your teeth play in digestion?
- What role does your tongue play in digestion?
- Which is longer, your small intestine or your large intestine?
- Which is wider, your small intestine or your large intestine?

TAKING IT FURTHER

- Can you eat or drink while standing on your head?
- Why do some foods spend 30 minutes in the stomach while other foods spend 3 hours in the stomach?
- What makes you feel hungry?
- Why did God design your body with a way to make you feel hungry?

CHEMICALS

As we already mentioned, digestion is primarily a chemical process. Glands in the mouth add an enzyme called salivary amylase to the food that begins breaking down the starch molecules in your food even while it is still in your mouth. But the real chemical reactions begin in the stomach. The lining of the stomach secretes various enzymes as well as hydrochloric acid and mucus. These liquids combined together are called gastric juice. The gastric juice softens the food and breaks down the proteins into molecules that can be absorbed by the body.

Additional chemicals are added to the food as it enters the small intestine. Some of the chemicals are produced by the liver and stored in the gall bladder until they are released into the small intestine. This liquid is called bile and its main function is to break down fat molecules into tiny droplets. Other chemicals are produced by the pancreas and squirted into the small intestine. Pancreatic juices contain many chemicals that help digest fats, proteins, and carbohydrates. The pancreas also produces sodium bicarbonate, the same chemical as baking soda, which neutralizes the hydrochloric acid from the stomach.

Without all these chemicals, our bodies could not extract the energy we need from our food. Thankfully, God has designed a wonderful system that efficiently provides all the energy we need.

Using an anatomy book, label all of the parts of the digestive system on the "Digestive System" worksheet.

TEETH

Grind that food

How many teeth do you have?

Words to know:

incisors

cuspids

canine teeth

bicuspids

molars

Challenge words:

crown

neck

root

pulp

root canal

dentin

enamel

cementum

periodontal ligament

gingiva

BEGINNERS

When you smile, you show your beautiful teeth to the world. Your teeth are important. Not only do they give you a nice smile, but they help you eat your food. You bite into food with your teeth and you chew your food into small enough pieces to swallow. This is the beginning of digestion.

God designed your mouth so that you grow two sets of teeth. You get your first tooth as a baby, so your first set of teeth are often called baby teeth. You have 20 baby teeth in all. As you get older, your mouth gets bigger but your teeth do not, so your baby teeth begin to fall out to make room for bigger teeth. Have you lost any teeth yet?

Your teeth are very important so you need to take care of them. We will learn more about taking care of your teeth in the next lesson.

- **How do your teeth help with digestion?**

- **How many sets of teeth will you have in your lifetime?**

- **Why do you have more than one set of teeth?**

T eeth are an important part of the digestive system. Without good healthy teeth it is difficult to enjoy any but the softest foods. God designed our mouths to have two sets of teeth. The first set of teeth begins emerging when you are a baby. These teeth are relatively small because your mouth is small. In all, you will have 20 baby teeth.

As you grow, your mouth gets larger, making room for more and bigger teeth. When you are around 6 or 7 years old, you may start losing your baby teeth. A tooth will become

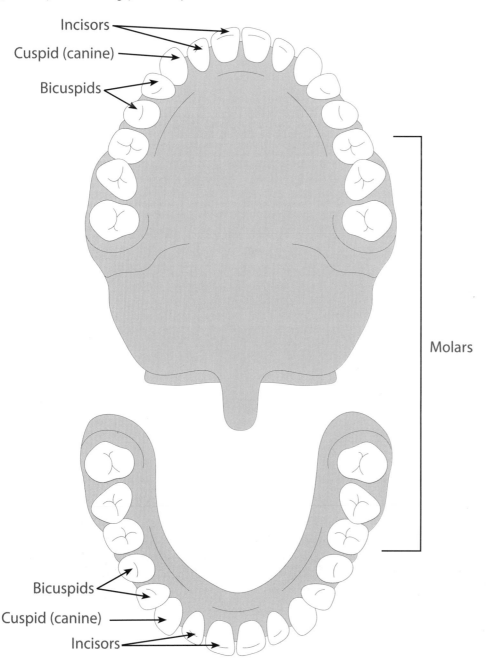

Incisors

Cuspid (canine)

Bicuspids

Molars

Bicuspids

Cuspid (canine)

Incisors

Digestion

TEETH MOLDS

Purpose: To get a good look at your own teeth

Materials: modeling clay, tag board, plaster of Paris, aluminum foil

Procedure:

1. Form some modeling clay into a cookie shape about ¾ inch thick that will fit inside your mouth and around your teeth.

2. Press the clay onto your upper teeth up to the gums and then carefully remove the clay. Repeat this process for your bottom teeth.

3. Cut a two-inch wide strip of tag board, wrap it snugly around the clay, and tape the ends together. This should form a collar around the clay to hold the plaster. Repeat this for each piece of clay.

4. In a small bowl or cup, mix enough water with a small amount of plaster of Paris to form a creamy liquid.

5. Place the clay molds on a piece of foil and pour a small amount of plaster into each clay mold and shake the molds gently to fill in all the cracks.

6. Pour in enough plaster to fill the mold about half way up the collar.

7. Allow the plaster to dry for at least 8 hours.

8. When the plaster is dry, gently remove the tag board and the clay.

Conclusion: What you end up with should look something like the chart on the previous page though you probably have fewer teeth. Name each tooth and review its function in the eating process.

loose and eventually fall out, making room for the larger permanent tooth. Also, as you continue to grow, additional teeth will grow in the back of your mouth that will not fall out. If all your teeth come in normally, you will have 32 teeth when you are an adult.

All of the teeth in your mouth are shaped differently and serve different functions. On the previous page is a chart showing the names of the teeth. In the front of your mouth are the incisors. **Incisors** have sharp straight edges for cutting and biting. On either side of the incisors are the **cuspids** or **canine teeth**. Canine teeth are pointed for tearing. Further back in the mouth are the bicuspids and molars. **Bicuspids** and **molars** are bumpy with a larger surface area for grinding. ■

FUN FACT

If you're right handed, you will usually chew your food on your right side. If you're left handed, you will tend to chew your food on your left side.

WHAT DID WE LEARN?

- What is the job of each kind of tooth?
- Why do people have baby teeth and why do they fall out?

TAKING IT FURTHER

- Why do we need to take care of our teeth?

TOOTH STRUCTURE

There are three parts to any tooth. The first part is the **crown**. This is the part of the tooth that you see. The crown is the part that helps you chew your food and allows you to have a beautiful smile. Below the crown is the part of the tooth called the neck. The **neck** goes down into your gums. Finally, the **root** of the tooth holds the tooth tightly in your jaw. When you lose your baby teeth, the roots of the teeth dissolve which is why they fall out.

If you look at a cross section of a tooth you see that the innermost part of the tooth is the pulp. The **pulp** contains nerves and blood vessels, which nourish the tooth and keep it healthy. These blood vessels enter the tooth at the tips of the roots and run up through the **root canals**. Surrounding the pulp is a substance called dentin. **Dentin** is a bonelike layer that gives the tooth its shape and size. Covering the dentin is a layer of enamel. **Enamel** is the hardest substance in the body and is comprised mostly of calcium and phosphorous.

The roots of the tooth are surrounded by a substance called **cementum**, which does exactly what it sounds like: it cements the tooth in place. Between the cementum and the jawbone itself is a fiber called the **periodontal ligament**, and above the jawbone is the **gingiva**, which you call your gums.

Although there is some controversy about whether fluoride should be added to drinking water, it is true that fluoride makes teeth stronger and more resistant to decay, and many cities add a fluoride compound to the water supply.

Fluoride reacts chemically with the enamel in the tooth to make it more resistant to decay. Before a tooth erupts, fluoride reacts with the dentin and pulp as well as the enamel; however, after the tooth comes in only the enamel reacts with the fluoride.

Use three different colors of modeling clay to make a cross-section model of a tooth. Be sure to review the function and name of each part of the tooth.

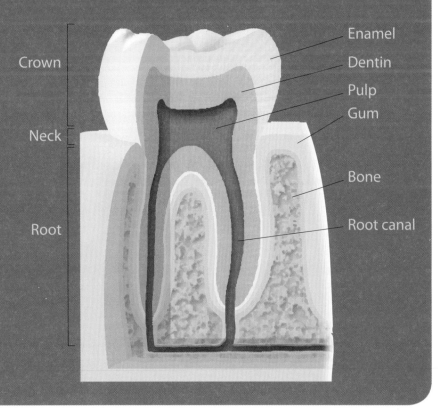

Crown
Neck
Root

Enamel
Dentin
Pulp
Gum
Bone
Root canal

Digestion

DENTAL HEALTH

Taking care of those teeth

LESSON 21

How do you properly care for your teeth?

Words to know:

plaque

Challenge words:

orthodontics

occlusion

retainer

BEGINNERS

Teeth are very important to eating, so you need to take good care of them. It is important that you brush your teeth at least twice a day. This helps to get rid of any bits of food that are stuck on your teeth and helps to keep you from getting cavities, which are tiny holes in your teeth. You should also use dental floss to clean out between your teeth every day. If you clean your teeth every day, it will help to keep your teeth healthy and strong.

You should also visit your dentist periodically to have your teeth cleaned even better than you can do at home. Dentists can also check for cavities and fix them before they get too big.

Finally, you need to eat and drink the right foods to keep your teeth healthy. If you eat healthy foods, your teeth will be strong. And if you keep sugary foods and drinks off of your teeth by brushing right after you eat or drink the sugary substance, this will help keep you from getting cavities.

- How often should you brush your teeth?

- Why should you go to the dentist regularly?

- What can you do besides brushing to help keep your teeth healthy?

Because teeth are so important to eating, it is important to take care of them. There are some very good reasons why your mom or dad makes you brush your teeth before you go to bed. Bacteria in your mouth break down sugars and form an acid. This is a natural part of the digestive process. However, these acids can attack the outside of your teeth and damage the enamel if they remain in your mouth too long. Brushing your teeth removes bits of food and helps keep the acids off of your teeth.

Sipping sugary drinks such as juice or soda over a long period of time, sucking on hard candy, or chewing sugary gum prolongs the time that sugar is in your mouth. These activities should be avoided. If you limit sugary foods and drinks to meal times, this helps reduce the amount of sugar in your mouth.

Also, a sticky substance called **plaque** builds up on the teeth. This not only traps the bacteria, sugar, and acid against the teeth, but it can also cause infection in the gums if it is not removed regularly. So, you should brush at least twice each day. You should also use dental floss to remove plaque from between your teeth each day. Finally, you should visit your dentist twice a year to have your teeth cleaned.

Eating healthy foods such as fruits and vegetables, and foods with calcium help strengthen your teeth. Especially avoid eating sticky, chewy foods that stick to your teeth. If you do eat sticky foods, you should brush your teeth right away. Developing good dental habits while you are young will help you keep your teeth healthy throughout your life. ■

PRACTICE, PRACTICE

Stand in front of a mirror and practice brushing your teeth. Have your teacher or parent demonstrate proper methods of brushing teeth. After you have adequately brushed, have them show you how to floss your teeth, and then get help flossing all your teeth. You may have already learned these things, but it never hurts to review these important skills.

If you are unsure how to brush or floss properly, you may contact a dentist (who will be happy to help teach you the proper methods for caring for your teeth).

WHAT DID WE LEARN?

- What are three things you can do to have healthy teeth?
- How does brushing your teeth help keep them healthy?
- List some foods that are good for your teeth.
- List some foods that are bad for your teeth.

TAKING IT FURTHER

- Since your baby teeth are going to fall out anyway, why do you still need to brush them and take care of them?

STRAIGHT TEETH

Many children and teenagers, and even some adults, have braces to help straighten teeth that do not come in straight or to correct jaw alignment. The practice of straightening teeth and correcting how they line up is called orthodontics. Attempts have been made to correct the way a person's teeth look for more than a thousand years; however, modern orthodontics began around 1850. To begin with, people attempted to correct poor tooth alignment by pulling teeth. Then in the 1890s they began replacing extracted teeth with false teeth to improve a person's appearance.

Also in the 1890s, Dr. Edward Angle developed a classification system for how teeth and jaws line up with each other. This system helped establish what would be considered a normal occlusion, or normal bite. Once orthodontists knew what was normal they developed ways to not only straighten the teeth but to also improve the alignment of the jaws.

Today, orthodontists use a variety of methods to correct crooked teeth and misaligned jaws. These methods include brackets attached to the teeth with wires between the brackets as wells as elastic bands, expanders, and headgear. Once a person's teeth and jaws are corrected, they usually wear a retainer to hold the teeth in the proper position until the bones around the teeth grow solid. A proper bite not only improves a person's looks, but also improves dental health.

Orthodontics is much more common today than it was only 20 to 30 years ago. Do a survey to find out how many people you know have had braces. Ask 10 adults and 10 young people and find out how many of them have had or currently have braces. You will probably find that a higher percentage of the young people have had braces than of the adults.

Digestion

NUTRITION

What should you eat?

What does a healthy diet look like?

Words to know:

carbohydrate

BEGINNERS

What are your favorite foods? Do you like cookies and candy? Are these the foods your mother is always encouraging you to eat? Probably not. Your mother probably encourages you to eat more fruits and vegetables and fewer sweets. This is because fruits and vegetables, cheese and yogurt, and many other foods, have more nutritional value. That means they give you more of what your body needs.

Foods have been divided into groups. One group contains bread, crackers, and cereal. Another group has fruits and vegetables. The next group has milk, cheese, and yogurt. And the last group has meat, fish, nuts, and dried beans. Each of these groups provides different things that your body needs, so you need to eat some of each group every day.

Did you notice that there weren't any cookies, candy, or soft drinks in these food groups? To keep your body healthy, you need to eat the foods in the food groups and only eat sweets in small amounts.

- **What are the four groups of food mentioned in this lesson?**

- **Why do you need to eat some of each group every day?**

- **Why shouldn't you eat too many sweets?**

The digestive system takes the food you eat and turns it into energy and nutrients for your body. But your body can only use what you feed it. Therefore, it is very important to eat the right foods and drink the right liquids so your body will have what it needs to grow strong and healthy. Eating too many sugary or high-fat foods can make you feel full and not willing to eat the foods that are better for you. Also, leaving out one of the food groups can prevent you from getting the vitamins and minerals your body needs. Thankfully, God has created a wide variety of foods. And people are very creative in preparing these foods so you can enjoy eating what your body needs.

To help you understand the different kinds of foods available, scientists have grouped foods together by the nutrients they supply to your body. The food groups include breads and grains, vegetables, fruits, dairy products, and meat and beans.

Breads and grains are high in **carbohydrates**, which are sugars and starches. Carbohydrates are a great source of energy. Foods in this category include whole wheat bread, oats, corn, cereals, rice, crackers, and pasta. You need to eat a significant amount of these kinds of foods each day.

Fruits and vegetables are probably the most important foods for you to eat. These foods are full of carbohydrates, vitamins, and minerals. Vegetables come in a wide variety of flavors, colors, and textures. Most can be enjoyed raw or cooked. Vegetables include broccoli, carrots, cucumbers, squash, green beans, peas, onions, tomatoes, lettuce, cabbage, beets, eggplant, and much more. Fruits are a sweet treat that can be eaten at any meal or as a healthy snack. Fruits include apples, pears, cherries, grapes, mangoes, strawberries, raspberries, pineapples, bananas, cranberries, grapefruit, lemons, oranges, and much more.

Many people, especially children, do not eat enough fruits and vegetables. You need to eat several servings of these healthy foods each day. Fresh or frozen fruits and vegetables almost always have more nutritional value than canned fruits and vegetables. You should eat a wide variety of fruits and vegetables. Eating the same vegetable or the same fruit every day will not give you all of the nutrients that you need.

The next food group is the dairy group. This includes foods such as milk, cheese, and yogurt. These products

Fun Fact

It can take more energy to digest celery than what you get from eating it, so a celery snack won't spoil your dinner!

EATING A HEALTHY MEAL

Plan a healthy lunch for you and your family. Be sure to select foods from all the different food groups. Arrange the food on each plate in a fun way. For example, you could make a face with the food by using broccoli pieces or carrot sticks to form a smile along the bottom of the plate, use apple slices for the ears, crackers with peanut butter for the eyes, and raisins for the nose. Add a glass of milk and you will have a creative and healthy meal.

provide calcium and protein for strong muscles and bones. Some people are concerned about getting too much fat from these products. You can limit the fat by drinking skim milk or eating low-fat cheese. But it is important to include dairy products so that you get the important nutrients that these foods provide.

The meat group includes beef, pork, fish, poultry, nuts, peanuts, and dried beans. All of these foods contain protein, which is needed for rapid growth and strong muscles. Again, variety is important so you receive all the different nutrients that your body needs.

If you look carefully through all the foods listed here, you will see that there are no cookies, potato chips, candy, soda, or other junk foods listed. These items are called junk food because they do not provide you with many nutrients and they are high in calories. They fill you up, but do not give you many of the building blocks that your body needs. You should limit the amount of sweets and fatty foods that you eat. It is okay to eat these foods in small amounts, but you should try to eat mostly foods that will help you grow strong and healthy. You are better off choosing a piece of fruit or some carrot sticks for a snack than a cookie or chips. ■

WHAT DID WE LEARN?

- What are the five food groups listed in this lesson?
- What types of foods should you eat only a small amount of each day?
- Why is variety in your diet important?

TAKING IT FURTHER

- Can a vegetarian eat a balanced diet? Hint: What other foods contain proteins found in meat?
- Is it necessary to eat dessert to have a healthy diet?

NUTRITION WORKSHEET

Complete the "Nutrition Worksheet" to get a better idea of why some foods are good for you and why others are not so good for you. You can probably find the needed information on food labels in your kitchen or on the Internet.

FLORENCE NIGHTINGALE

1820–1910

The profession of nursing as we know it today owes much to one remarkable lady—Florence Nightingale. She is considered to be the first real nurse in England, and she became famous because she took other women to a war zone to help those who were wounded. But have you ever wanted to know why she did what she did? It was because God called her to do it.

Florence was born in Florence, Italy in 1820. She and her family returned to their home in England the next year. The Nightingales were a very wealthy family. Florence received most of her education at home from her father.

When Florence was almost 17 years old, she sensed God speaking to her, calling her to His service. But she was not sure how He wanted her to serve Him. From that time on she looked for ways to serve God. For several years Florence sought advice about how she could serve the poor and hurting people around her. In 1842 she learned about an orphanage and hospital in Germany where trained nurses were taking care of the poor in clean hospitals. This was a new idea to her, and she began to think about becoming a nurse.

After prayerfully considering her decision, Florence told her parents that she had decided to become a nurse. At this time, women of culture and education did not work as nurses. Nursing was only done by the poor and outcasts of society. Her parents were horrified. Her parents, hoping to change Florence's mind, encouraged her to go on a trip through Europe. But while on that trip, Florence studied what other countries were doing to help the sick and the poor, and she became an expert on hospitals and sanitation.

In 1851 Florence decided to begin formal nurse's training and went to Kaiserwerth in Germany. This was the hospital she had heard about many years before. For four months she learned how to care for the sick and to treat many diseases. She then continued her education in Paris where Catholic nuns taught her more about nursing the sick.

In 1853 Florence felt that God wanted her to work serving the "sick poor" in England. She was offered the position as superintendent of The Institute for the Care of Sick Gentlewomen in Distressed Circumstances. This was a hospital in England that treated servants of wealthy people. Florence gladly accepted. Finally, she would be able to help in her home country.

The following year, England, France, and Sardinia came to the aid of Turkey in a war against Russia. The public heard of the needs of the wounded soldiers through the newspaper. They were outraged to find that their wounded soldiers were not being taken care of. Sidney Herbert, the Secretary of War, asked Florence to go help the wounded British soldiers, and she felt God calling her to this task. Florence put together a group of 38 nurses and went to Turkey. She was told that the hospital was a splendid facility and had an abundance of supplies. But what she found was quite different. She found a horribly dirty hospital where the wounded were surrounded by filth. There were no supplies, and the doctors were completely overwhelmed.

Florence went right to work. She instituted many changes to benefit the soldiers. Often the doctors opposed her changes. Many of them did not think women should be nurses and none of them liked taking orders from a nurse. But Florence insisted on implementing what she had learned and the results were spectacular. The death rate dropped from 42% to 2% in only five months. Florence and her nurses emerged from the war as heroines to both the soldiers and the people back home.

However, this victory was not without cost. Florence came down with what was called Crimean Fever. Some people believe this may have been Post Traumatic Stress Disorder. She was never strong physically again. She spent most of the rest of her life secluded and often in bed.

Her physical condition did not stop her desire to see improvements in the medical field, however. In 1859 she published a booklet entitled "Notes on Nursing." Millions of copies were sold, and the royalties from the book were the only wages Florence ever received.

Then, in 1860, the Nightingale Training School for nurses opened in London. Fifteen women began the one-year course and thirteen graduated. This school is considered the start of modern nursing, and completely changed the image of female nursing.

In 1861 Florence was asked to set up a plan to care for the sick and wounded of the American Civil War. She sent helpful information to the American Secretary of War and to Dorothea Dix, Superintendent of Nurses for Union forces.

Florence made many important changes to the hospital system in England as well. She set up separate wards for men, women, children, and the insane. She insisted that patients be given bells so they could ring for a nurse when they needed attention. She insisted on sanitary conditions. These changes spread throughout Europe and in 1872, Henri Durant, the founder of the Red Cross, said Florence's work had influenced him greatly.

When Florence was 76 years old, she was confined to bed permanently. At the age of 87, the King of England bestowed on her the "Order of Merit." She was the first woman to receive this high honor. She died in 1910, and at her burial six sergeants of the British Army carried her coffin.

Florence Nightingale followed God's calling on her life, and as a result millions of lives have been saved.

VITAMINS & MINERALS

Do I have to go to a
mine to get minerals?

LESSON 23

**Where can you
find the vitamins
and minerals
needed for a
healthy body?**

BEGINNERS

As you learned in the last lesson, you need to eat different kinds of foods because different foods provide different things that your body needs. Some of the things that are provided by the different foods are called vitamins and minerals. Vitamins are usually given letter names such as vitamin A or vitamin C. Eggs and milk give your body vitamin A, and oranges and tomatoes give your body vitamin C. Other foods have different vitamins, so you need to eat different foods so you can get all the vitamins your body needs.

Foods also contain minerals that often have names that sound like metals. One mineral that your body needs is iron. You don't want to eat a nail to get iron, but you can eat meat or dried beans to get the iron you need. You get calcium from milk and cheese, and potassium from bananas.

- What are two things you can get from your food that you learned about in this lesson?

- What kind of names are given to vitamins?

- How can you make sure you get the vitamins and minerals your body needs?

Foods contain energy in one of three forms: carbohydrates (sugars and starches), proteins, and fats. The digestive system breaks food down so your body can get energy from it. It uses different chemicals from the liver, pancreas, and gallbladder to break down these different forms of food.

Food also contains vitamins and minerals that your body needs. If you eat a wide variety of foods that have not been processed, you should get all of the vitamins and minerals you need. However, many processed foods no longer contain their original nutrients. Therefore, many foods have vitamins and minerals added to them.

Some of the vitamins you need and some of the foods that contain them include:

Vitamin A—found in eggs, milk, dark green vegetables

Vitamin B complex—found in wheat germ, brown rice, meat, milk, most vegetables

Vitamin C—found in citrus fruits, tomatoes, broccoli, green peppers

Vitamin D—found in milk, salmon, tuna, eggs

Vitamin E—found in whole grain bread, cabbage, lettuce, yeast

Vitamin K—found in yogurt, dark green leafy vegetables, cabbage, eggs

Your body also needs many minerals. Most of these are needed in very small amounts. Some of the minerals you need in slightly larger amounts include:

Calcium—found in dairy products

Iron—found in meat, dried beans, breads, cereals

Magnesium—found in whole grains, potatoes, fruits

Phosphorus—found in milk, cheese, dried beans

Sodium—found in salt, milk, tomatoes, celery, meat

Potassium—found in bananas and other fruits, soybeans, mushrooms, breads

By eating a wide variety of foods, you will get the vitamins and minerals your body needs.

Finally, one of the most important substances that you need for good health is water. Your body is about 60% water. Every cell contains water. Water is used in nearly every function of the body. So it is vital to restore the water in the body every-

FUN FACT

Your brain is composed of 70% water, your lungs are nearly 90% water, and 83% of your blood is water.

FUN FACT

Women are more likely to need vitamin and mineral supplements than men are. A woman's body needs more calcium and vitamin D to maintain healthy bones than a man's body does. So women, especially once they reach the age of 40, are often encouraged to take supplements to keep their bodies healthy.

VITAMIN & MINERAL SCAVENGER HUNT

Purpose: To find as many of the vitamins and minerals listed in this lesson as you can

Materials: food containers

Procedure:

1. Take a look at several cans and boxes of food in your kitchen. By law, every package of food must be labeled with certain nutritional information. This includes serving size and servings per container, calories, grams of fat, carbohydrates and protein, and certain vitamins and minerals.

2. See how many of the vitamins and minerals listed in this lesson you can find in the foods on the shelves of your kitchen. Breakfast cereals almost always have added vitamins and minerals, so that is an easy place to start.

3. After checking out a variety of foods, write out a menu for at least three meals, including breakfast, lunch, and dinner.

4. Show how many servings from each section of the food pyramid have been included and which vitamins and minerals are included. Remember, many foods fit into more than one category on the pyramid. For example, yogurt with fruit in it is dairy and fruit. A peanut butter and jelly sandwich would be meat, bread, and possibly fruit (although most jelly is primarily sugar and has very little real fruit in it).

day. The amount of water needed varies depending on your size and activity level, the foods you eat, and the temperature outside. Some water comes from the foods we eat, but to be healthy most children should drink about six glasses of water every day. To avoid getting too much sugar and salt, water is a better choice than soda pop. ■

WHAT DID WE LEARN?

- What are the three main types of compounds found in food?
- How can we be sure to get enough vitamins and minerals in our diet?
- Why is water so important to our diet?

TAKING IT FURTHER

- Can you drink soda instead of water?
- Are frozen dinners just as healthy as fresh food?
- Is restaurant food as healthy as home-cooked food?

HEALTH PROBLEMS

A lack of a particular vitamin or mineral in your diet can lead to serious health problems. For each of the following diseases, find out what causes that disease, what the symptoms are, and how to prevent it.

- Scurvy
- Rickets
- Anemia
- Goiter

UNIT 5

HEART & LUNGS

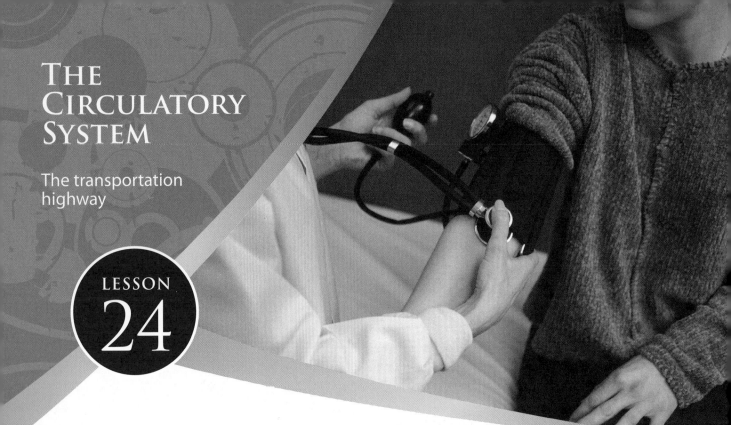

THE CIRCULATORY SYSTEM

The transportation highway

LESSON 24

How many directions does blood flow in your body?

Words to know:

circulatory system

artery

vein

capillary

Challenge words:

blood pressure

systolic blood pressure

diastolic blood pressure

BEGINNERS

One of the most important parts of your body is your **circulatory system**. This is the part of your body that moves your blood around. You can remember the name of this system if you think that circulatory sounds like circle and remember that the blood moves from your heart to all the parts of your body and back to the heart in something like a big circle.

The blood takes food and oxygen to every part of your body. This is how your body gets energy and is able to keep working. The blood also picks up things your body doesn't need, like carbon dioxide, and takes them away from the various parts of the body to where they can leave the body.

Your heart is what makes the blood move. Your heart is a muscle that acts like a pump to push the blood to the rest of your body. First the heart pushes blood to the lungs where carbon dioxide leaves the blood and oxygen enters the blood. This blood returns to your heart and is then pushed throughout the rest of the body. One of the places the blood flows is around your small intestine where food is absorbed into the blood to be taken to all the other parts of the body.

- What is the name of the system that moves your blood around?

- What part of your body pushes the blood around?

- What are two things that the blood takes to all the parts of the body?

- What is one thing that the blood takes away from the parts of the body?

The transportation highway of your body is the **circulatory system**. This system is made up of your heart, blood, and blood vessels. Your heart is really a magnificent pump, which pushes the blood throughout your entire body. This highway transports needed materials to each cell and carts away waste materials. The red blood cells are like trucks, the valves in the blood vessels are like traffic signals, and oxygen and carbon dioxide are some of the cargo that gets transported.

Blood is pushed out of the heart into the lungs where the red blood cells receive oxygen and give up carbon dioxide. This blood then returns to the heart where it is pumped throughout the body. As the blood passes through the digestive system, it absorbs food and nutrients to carry to the rest of the body. As it deposits nutrients and oxygen in the body's cells, it picks up carbon dioxide and other waste products that will be eliminated by the lungs and kidneys.

Each time the blood circulates from the heart out to the body, about 20% of it goes through the kidneys. The kidneys filter out some of the waste before the blood heads back to the heart.

Your heart pushes your blood 24 hours a day, 7 days a week, every day of the year, and you don't even have to think about it. Your blood makes about 600 round trips from your heart to the other parts of the body each day. If other body systems quit working, your body can often compensate. You can survive for many days without eating and some people live their whole lives without being able to see or hear. But you can only live a few minutes without your heart pumping oxygen-rich blood throughout your body.

FUN FACT

The body contains approximately 25 trillion red blood cells. Each red blood cell lives about 120 days before it must be replaced. Therefore, the marrow in your long bones keeps very busy producing 2 million red blood cells every second!

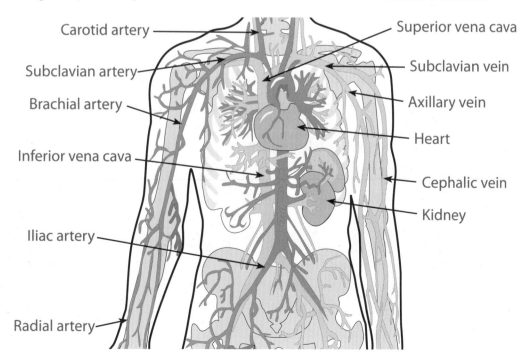

Carotid artery

Subclavian artery

Brachial artery

Inferior vena cava

Iliac artery

Radial artery

Superior vena cava

Subclavian vein

Axillary vein

Heart

Cephalic vein

Kidney

Heart & Lungs

MEASURING YOUR PULSE

Your pulse is the number of times your heart beats each minute. There are several places where you can feel your pulse. The most commonly used location is on your wrist, just up your arm from your thumb joint. Another place is on your thumb. (Don't use your thumb to feel someone else's pulse, you just might be feeling your own instead.) A third place that you can easily feel your pulse is either side of your neck, just below your jaw. You can feel your pulse in these areas because these blood vessels are near the surface and are large enough for you to feel the surge of blood each time your heart beats.

Purpose: To test the effects of exercise on your heartbeat

Materials: stopwatch

Procedure:

1. Sit still for five minutes

2. Find your pulse and, using a stopwatch, count how many times your heart beats in 15 seconds.

3. Multiply that number by 4 to estimate your resting heart rate (beats per minute).

4. Next, exercise for 5 minutes by running in place or doing jumping jacks.

5. Now measure your pulse again.

6. Finally, rest for 5 minutes and measure your pulse again. What did you notice about your pulse?

As blood travels throughout your body, it goes through three kinds of blood vessels. **Arteries** carry blood away from the heart. **Veins** carry blood toward the heart. **Capillaries** are the very small vessels connecting veins with arteries. This is where the blood exchanges oxygen for carbon dioxide. Capillaries are so small that the red blood cells must go through single file—one at a time. On the previous page is a diagram showing some of the veins and arteries in your body.

Blood can only flow in one direction through the heart because valves inside it only open in one direction. When the heart contracts, blood is pushed through these valves, then when the heart rests, the valves close and the blood cannot flow back. God has truly created an amazing system for nourishing every cell in your body. ■

WHAT DID WE LEARN?

- What are the three main parts of the circulatory system?
- What are two functions of blood?
- What are three types of blood vessels?
- Which blood vessels carry blood away from the heart?
- Which blood vessels carry blood toward the heart?
- What happens to the blood in the capillaries?

TAKING IT FURTHER

- How is the circulatory system like a highway?
- Why is exercise important for your circulatory system?
- List two other systems that depend on the circulatory system to function properly.
- Why does your pulse increase when you exercise?

Heart & Lungs

BLOOD PRESSURE

Have you ever heard someone say they have high blood pressure? You many not know what that really means. **Blood pressure** refers to the pressure placed on the walls of the blood vessels as they carry the blood throughout the body. This pressure is what keeps the blood moving.

The pressure in your blood vessels is not constant. If you are sleeping, your blood pressure will be lower than when you are exercising. The pressure also changes as your heart beats and then rests. When the ventricles in your heart squeeze the blood out, the pressure in your blood vessels goes up. This is called **systolic blood pressure**. When your heart rests, the pressure in your vessels goes down. This is called **diastolic blood pressure**. The ratio of the systolic over diastolic pressure is referred to as your blood pressure.

This blood pressure is measured in units called millimeters of mercury or mmHg. The normal range for systolic blood pressure is 110–140 mmHg and the normal range for diastolic pressure is 60–90 mmHg. So a normal blood pressure might be 120 over 80, written as120/80. If either number is above the normal range, that person is said to have high blood pressure.

High blood pressure puts stress on the heart and can cause many health problems. Therefore, people with high blood pressure often have special diets and exercise programs to help lower their pressure, or they may take medication to keep their blood pressure under control.

If you have a chance, find out what your blood pressure is. You can have your blood pressure measured at a doctor's office or clinic.

Heart & Lungs

THE HEART

Master pump

LESSON 25

Why does your heart need valves and chambers?

Words to know:

atrium

ventricle

pulmonary artery

pulmonary vein

hemoglobin

BEGINNERS

Your circulatory system would not work without your heart. Your heart is a very strong muscle. Your heart is so important that God placed it in the middle of your chest where it is protected by your ribs.

Your heart has four chambers which are like little rooms. The top chambers are called the left **atrium** and right atrium, and the bottom chambers are called the left **ventricle** and the right ventricle. Blood enters the top of the heart, then flows into the bottom of the heart where it is squeezed out to go to other parts of the body.

Your heart works very hard for you. It pumps all day long and all night long. It never stops. But it does rest in between beats. God designed your heart to be strong enough to pump all the time for your whole life. You can make your heart even stronger by exercising. Aren't you glad God gave you such a special heart?

• **What is the part of your body that pumps your blood?**

• **How was your body designed to protect your heart?**

• **What can you do to make your heart stronger?**

The heart is the major organ of the circulatory system and one of the most important organs in your entire body. That is why God designed it to rest inside your rib cage surrounded by a layer of fat where it is protected from the outside world. The heart is a very strong muscle that contracts and relaxes about 70 times each minute for adults and more often for children. When the heart contracts it pushes blood out and when it relaxes it allows blood to flow into it.

The human heart is designed with four sections or chambers. The upper chambers are the left **atrium** and right atrium and the lower chambers are the left and right **ventricles**. Blood from the body enters the right atrium and then flows into the right ventricle. It is pushed from the right ventricle through the **pulmonary artery** to the lungs where it receives oxygen and gets rid of carbon dioxide. The oxygen-rich blood then returns to the left atrium through the **pulmonary veins** and then flows into the left ventricle. It then leaves the left ventricle to go to the rest of the body.

Your heart pumps blood through about 60,000 miles (96,500 km) of blood vessels. Though your heart beats 24 hours a day, 7 days a week, it also gets to rest in between each contraction. So, it actually is working less than half of the time.

Since your heart is a muscle you can make it stronger by exercising it. Doing regular exercise a few times each week makes your heart stronger so it doesn't have to work as hard the rest of the time. ■

WHAT DID WE LEARN?

- What are the four chambers of the heart?
- How many times does a blood cell pass through the heart on each trip around the body?

TAKING IT FURTHER

- What are some things you can do to help your heart stay healthy?
- Is your heart shaped like a valentine?
- Does Jesus live in your physical heart?

BLOOD FLOW IN THE HEART

A chemical in red blood cells, called hemoglobin, is what makes these cells red. Hemoglobin turns bright red when it reacts with oxygen. When oxygen leaves the blood cells and enters the surrounding tissues, the red blood cells lose their bright red color and turn a dark red.

Fill out "The Heart" worksheet. Color blood containing oxygen red and blood containing carbon dioxide blue. Review the flow of blood through the heart.

Remember that blood flowing from the body into the heart and lungs should be colored blue even though your blood is never really blue (see Fun Fact), and blood flowing from the lungs and out of the heart to the rest of the body should be red.

EXAMINE A HEART

Mammals such as sheep and cattle have a four-chambered heart similar to a human heart. You can learn a lot about how the human heart looks and works by examining a cow's heart. You can obtain a cow's heart from your local grocery store or butcher. If you prefer, you can order a preserved cow's heart or sheep heart from a science supply store.

For those of you who are too squeamish to actually dissect a heart, you can view a dissection online at several different web sites. One possible web site is: http://learning.mgccc.cc.ms.us/science/heart2/sld001.htm. This web site is also a good

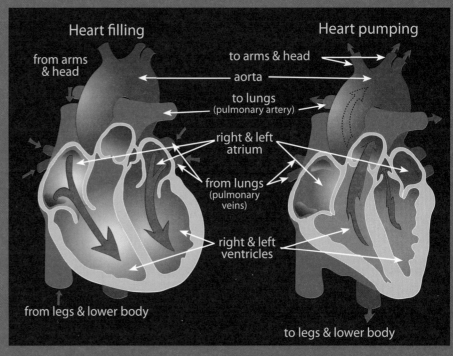

Heart filling

from arms & head

Heart pumping

to arms & head

aorta

to lungs (pulmonary artery)

right & left atrium

from lungs (pulmonary veins)

right & left ventricles

from legs & lower body

to legs & lower body

reference to have available even if you are not too squeamish for dissections. It provides a labeled

reference so you know what you are looking at.

Purpose: To dissect a heart

Materials: cow or sheep heart, knife, anatomy book

Procedure:

1. Be sure to use gloves when handling the heart. Examine the outside of the heart. Look for the veins and arteries where the blood enters and leaves the heart.

2. Squeeze the heart and see if you can feel the chambers.

3. Carefully cut open the heart. Look for each of the four chambers. Look also for the valves that keep the blood flowing in the right direction through the heart. You can use an anatomy book or a dissection guide as a reference to help you locate all the various parts of the heart (also see the diagram here).

FUN FACT

Why do the veins on your arms and hands appear blue? Do you have blue blood? The blue color you see is due to an optical effect caused by the way in which light penetrates through the skin. This has led to a common belief that the oxygen-depleted blood in our veins is blue. The blood in your veins is not blue, it just appears that way. It is actually a dark red.

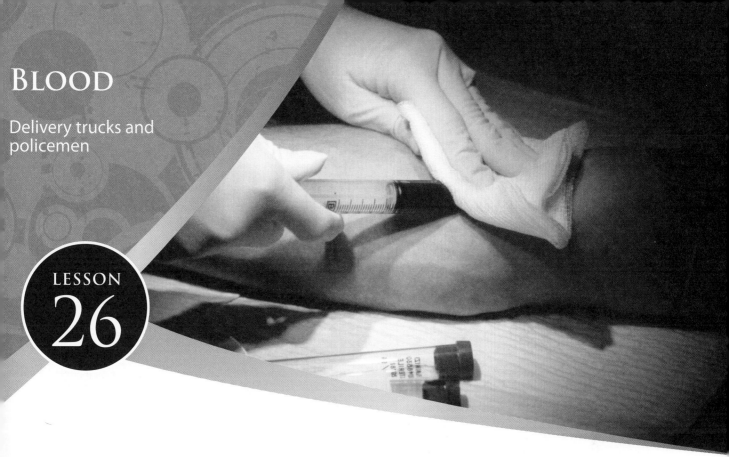

BLOOD

Delivery trucks and policemen

LESSON

26

How many different parts are found in your blood?

Words to know:

plasma

red blood cell

white blood cell

platelet

fibrin

Challenge words:

antigen

blood type

universal donor

universal recipient

BEGINNERS

Your blood contains four important ingredients. The first ingredient is called **plasma**. Plasma is a yellowish liquid that all the blood cells float in. The second ingredient is red blood cells. **Red blood cells** look like small round disks. These cells carry oxygen and food to the body and carry away carbon dioxide.

The third ingredient in blood is white blood cells. **White blood cells** help protect you from germs that get inside your body. If something gets into your body that should not be there, such as a germ, white blood cells quickly surround it and get rid of it so it cannot hurt you. This helps to keep you from getting sick.

The last ingredient in blood is the **platelets**. When you get a cut, these little cells rush to the cut and help seal it off so you don't bleed for too long. Platelets help form a scab so your cut can heal. All of these parts of blood help keep you healthy and strong.

- **What is plasma?**
- **What are the two kinds of blood cells in your blood?**
- **What do platelets do?**

If the circulatory system is a transportation highway, then your blood cells are the delivery trucks, construction workers, and policemen. Blood is made up of four parts. Fifty-five percent of your blood is **plasma**. This is a yellowish liquid that carries the blood cells through the blood vessels. Red blood cells make up 44.5% of your blood. **Red blood cells** are the delivery trucks that carry oxygen and nutrients to your cells and carry away waste products. The last 0.5% is made up of white blood cells and platelets. **White blood cells** are the policemen of the highway.

BLOOD CELL GAME

Purpose: To model the role of blood cells

Materials: chairs, construction paper

Red blood cells—Procedure:

1. Set chairs in two rows to represent the blood vessel.

2. Have the chairs become closer at one end to represent a capillary.

3. Set pieces of blue construction paper on the capillary chairs.

4. Have several people pretend to be red blood cells by holding red pieces of paper.

5. Go through the capillary one at a time and set down the red paper and pick up a blue paper. This represents the exchange of oxygen and carbon dioxide.

White blood cells and platelets—Procedure:

1. Some of you pretend to be white blood cells and others pretend to be platelets. One person should pretend to be a germ.

2. The germ starts outside the chairs and, when a break is made in the line of chairs, the germ enters the blood vessel.

3. The white blood cells surround the germ and take it back outside the vessel while the platelets rush to the opening and form a wall to prevent other germs from entering.

MAKING "SAMPLE" BLOOD

As you learned in the lesson, blood is made up of approximately 55% plasma, 44.5% red blood cells, 0.25% white blood cells, and 0.25% platelets. You can visualize this mixture by making your own sample blood.

Purpose: To make a "sample" of blood

Materials: corn syrup, red-hot candies, white jelly beans, candy sprinkles

Procedure:

1. Pour ½ cup corn syrup into a bowl. This represents the plasma.

2. Add ½ cup red-hot candies. This represents the red blood cells in your blood.

3. Add 1 tablespoon of white jelly beans, representing the white blood cells, and 1 tablespoon of candy sprinkles representing the platelets.

4. Mix these ingredients together and you have sample blood. What is the main color of your mixture? It should be red just like your real blood because of all the red blood cells.

If anything enters the body that does not belong, such as a germ, the white blood cells surround and eliminate it to help prevent infection and illness. The **platelets** are the highway construction crew. If there is a break in the highway, like when you cut your finger or skin your knee, platelets go to the break and stick together to close the cut. Then a stringy substance called **fibrin** forms a web over the cut and traps red blood cells in the web. This hardens into a scab and protects the area until the cut is healed. This keeps blood from escaping and germs from entering.

The body has approximately 25 trillion red blood cells. These cells are very tiny and very efficient. As red blood cells age they become stiff and less efficient, so they must be replaced. New red blood cells are generated in the bone marrow found in the center of long bones. The spleen and liver break down the old red blood cells, and their parts such as hemoglobin and iron are recycled to be used in making new red blood cells. Blood, with its ability to bring oxygen to every cell in the body, is perhaps the most essential part of your body. ■

A scanning electron micrograph of human blood, showing red blood cells (large disk-shaped), white blood cells (round), and platelets (small disk-shaped)

WHAT DID WE LEARN?

- What are the four parts of blood and the function of each part?
- What does your body do to help protect itself if you get cut?
- Do you have more red or white blood cells?

TAKING IT FURTHER

- What are some of the dangers of a serious cut?

Heart & Lungs

BLOOD TRANSFUSIONS

If someone has a serious injury and loses a large amount of blood, it may be necessary to give that person a blood transfusion to save her life. However, though all blood contains the same basic ingredients, all blood is not the same. Red blood cells contain certain information that makes it so your body recognizes your own cells and distinguishes them from invaders. Blood that will be accepted by the person's body must be used in the transfusion. If the wrong blood type is used, the person's body will attack the blood cells and this could result in death.

The first recorded blood transfusion took place in the 1660s when a man named Richard Lower tried transfusing blood between dogs. He had some success so he tried transfusing lamb's blood into a human. The patient died and blood transfusions were outlawed for some time. Then in 1818 a man named James Blundell performed the first successful blood transfusion between a husband and a wife. However, some of his other patients died. Doctors and scientists did not really understand why. Finally, in 1901 Karl Landsteiner discovered that red blood cells carry **antigens**, which are like identification tags on the cells. These antigens are called antigen A and antigen B. The presence or absence of these antigens determines a person's **blood type**.

Someone with blood type A has blood that contains only antigen A. His blood contains antibodies (substances that attack and destroy invaders), which attack antigen B cells. Someone with blood type B has only antigen B and has antibodies that attack antigen A. Some people have both antigens A and B in their blood and do not have any antibodies against other blood types. These people have type AB blood. Other people have neither A nor B antigens and are said to have type O blood. These people have antibodies that will attack both A and B blood cells. It is vitally important to determine the blood type of both the donor and the recipient before a blood transfusion takes place, to ensure that there will not be a problem.

Approximately 43% of the people in the world have type O blood, 40% have type A, 12% have type B, and 5% have type AB blood.

In addition to the antigens that determine the four major blood types, blood can also contain another tag called the rhesus factor, or Rh factor. If the blood contains this antigen, the person is said to be Rh positive. If the blood does not contain it, they are said to be Rh negative. So a person's blood type could be O positive or A negative, or any other combination. People who are Rh negative have antibodies that fight cells that are Rh positive. So someone that is Rh negative must have blood that is Rh negative, but someone that is Rh positive can receive blood that is either Rh positive or Rh negative. Approximately 85% of the general population is Rh positive. There are other identification tags that vary from person to person, but other tags generally do not cause the serious problems that the ones mentioned here can cause when blood types are mixed.

Given what you just learned, fill out the "Blood Types 1" worksheet showing which type or types of blood can *donate* to each blood type and which type or types of blood can be *received* by each blood type.

Next, fill out the "Blood Types 2" worksheet where we incorporate the Rh factor.

Which blood type is the **universal donor** (can donate to anyone)? Which blood type is the **universal recipient** (can receive any type of blood)?

BLOOD—WHO NEEDS IT?

Today we know that blood is one of the most important fluids in the body. It takes oxygen and nourishment to every part of the body, and removes waste products. The white blood cells also protect the body from infection. We also know today that without enough blood a person cannot live. However, people have not always understood this.

It has only been in the last 200 years that we have learned the importance of blood. Prior to that, blood was thought of as useless and in some cases harmful. Many illnesses were believed to be caused by "bad blood" or too much blood. In order to heal the person, the doctors would remove blood from the body. "Let out the blood, let out the disease," was a common motto for doctors until the nineteenth century.

The procedure known as bleeding (or blood-letting) was performed as a remedy for many different symptoms. Often the doctor would call in a barber to bleed the person. The barber would cut a vein or artery to let out the blood. Sometimes barbers would use leeches to suck out the bad blood. Barbers advertised their services with a red and white striped pole in front of their shops. Even though barbers no longer perform medical procedures, they have retained the red and white striped pole in many locations. The practice of using leeches to bleed people led to barbers, and sometimes doctors, being called leeches themselves.

Many patients were harmed and some even died as a result of being bled. George Washington, America's first president, is believed to have died because of blood-letting. President Washington originally had a cold. As he became more seriously ill, his doctors bled him. As he got worse they decided to let out more of the disease by bleeding him again. It is believed that this may have been the actual cause of his death. In the years prior to the 19th century, a person usually had a better chance of surviving using home remedies rather than seeing a doctor.

Understanding of the human body and the practice of medicine have improved dramatically in the last two hundred years. Today, you as a child might know more about the human body than doctors knew 200 to 300 years ago. And you certainly understand the importance of blood better than they did.

THE RESPIRATORY SYSTEM

A breath of fresh air

LESSON 27

How does oxygen get into your bloodstream?

Words to know:

respiratory system

diaphragm

pharynx

trachea

larynx

bronchi

bronchial tubes

alveoli

Challenge words:

respiration

external respiration

internal respiration

cellular respiration

BEGINNERS

Take a deep breath and hold it as long as you can. Why did you have to let your breath out? Your body needs oxygen to function and it gets that oxygen from the air you breathe. So you can't go very long without breathing.

The part of your body responsible for breathing is your **respiratory system**. This system includes your nose, throat, and lungs. Air enters your lungs, and oxygen from the air enters the blood that is in your lungs. Carbon dioxide from the blood enters the air and leaves your body when you let your breath out.

You don't have to think about breathing. You do it automatically. You can hold your breath for a little while, but eventually, your body will start breathing again.

- What are the major organs that you use when you breathe?
- What is the main purpose for breathing?
- What substance leaves your body when you breathe out?

Although the respiratory system is considered separate from the circulatory system, it is vitally connected to it. The circulatory system's main function is to get oxygen to the body. The **respiratory system's** main function is to get the oxygen to the blood. It does this through a series of "pipes" that go into the lungs and branch out like a tree's branches.

When you take a breath, a muscle below your lungs, called the **diaphragm**, contracts. This causes your chest to expand, drawing air into your lungs. The air goes through your nose and nasal passage, or through your mouth, and into the back of your throat, sometimes called the **pharynx**. There it enters a tube called the **trachea**, and then passes through the **larynx** or voice box. Below the larynx, the trachea splits into two tubes called **bronchi**, or bronchial tubes, which enter the lungs.

Inside the lungs the **bronchial tubes** split into many smaller tubes. At the end of each tube is a small sac called an alveolus. Capillaries surround the **alveoli**. Here, in these capillaries, the oxygen in the air is exchanged with the carbon dioxide in the blood. The oxygen enters the bloodstream to be taken throughout the body, and the carbon dioxide enters the air, which leaves your lungs as you exhale.

Breathing is an automatic function. You don't have to think

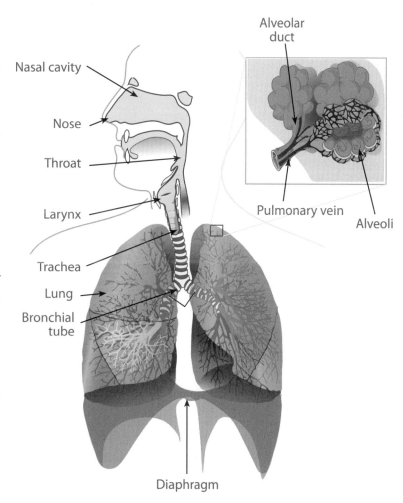

Nasal cavity

Nose

Throat

Larynx

Trachea

Lung

Bronchial tube

Diaphragm

Alveolar duct

Pulmonary vein

Alveoli

FUN FACT

Women's vocal cords are generally shorter than men's so they vibrate faster. This gives most women a higher voice than most men. On the average, women's vocal cords vibrate about 220 times per second, whereas men's vocal cords vibrate about 120 times per second when they are speaking.

RESPIRATORY SYSTEM WORKSHEET

Fill out "The Respiratory System" worksheet.

about it. Your brain responds to the amount of carbon dioxide in your blood, causing the diaphragm to contract and allowing air to enter your lungs. When the diaphragm relaxes, air is pushed from your lungs. You can consciously control your diaphragm to some extent, but if you try to stop breathing too long, your brain will force you to begin breathing again. ■

WHAT DID WE LEARN?

- Describe the breathing process.
- How do the circulatory and respiratory systems work together?
- Where inside the lungs does the exchange of gases occur?
- What are the major parts of the respiratory system?

TAKING IT FURTHER

- How do you suppose your body keeps food from going into your lungs and air from going into your stomach when both enter your body in the back of your throat?
- How does your respiratory system respond when you exercise?
- How does your respiratory system respond when you are sleeping?

RESPIRATION

When we think of respiration we think of breathing, and respiration definitely occurs when we breathe, but respiration does not always refer to breathing. **Respiration** is the exchange of oxygen and carbon dioxide. There are really several levels or types of respiration. The process of breathing is called external respiration. **External respiration** is the exchanging of oxygen for carbon dioxide in the lungs. This exchange occurs between the air and the blood in the lungs. **Internal respiration** occurs when oxygen and carbon dioxide are exchanged between blood cells and surrounding tissue cells. Finally, **cellular respiration** occurs when the gases are exchanged within a cell.

Cellular respiration is where the real action is. Inside the cell, oxygen is combined with food molecules to release the energy stored in the food molecules. The by-product of this chemical reaction is carbon dioxide. This is the process that provides energy for all living plants and animals.

We generally associate respiration with animals and photosynthesis with plants. Animals need oxygen, and plants produce oxygen through photosynthesis. However, plants also perform cellular respiration, especially at night when the sun is not shining, to get the energy they need to grow.

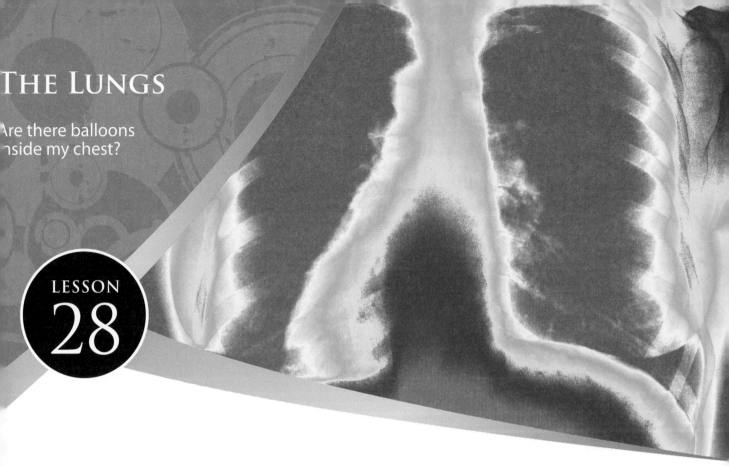

THE LUNGS

Are there balloons inside my chest?

LESSON

28

What does the inside of a lung look like?

Words to know:

asthma

cilia

pneumonia

BEGINNERS

You may think that your lungs are just like balloons that are empty until you fill them with air. But the inside of your lung really looks more like a tree with hollow branches. The tubes going into your lungs start out fairly large. Then they divide into smaller and smaller tubes until they finally end in tiny sacs. So the inside of your lung is really full of millions of tiny air sacs. You can look at the drawings in the previous lesson to get an idea of how the inside of your lungs look.

Having healthy lungs is very important. Sometimes people get sick and have difficulty breathing. Some people have **asthma**, which is a condition that makes the tubes in the lungs get smaller so it is harder to breathe. But one of the worst things that people do to hurt their lungs is to smoke cigarettes. You should do everything you can to keep your lungs healthy.

- If you could look inside your lungs would they look like balloons?

- What is at the end of the tubes inside your lungs?

- What is something you can do to keep your lungs healthy?

Because lungs inflate and deflate like a balloon, people often think their lungs are just like balloons—empty inside until you take a breath. But this is not the case. As we learned in the last lesson, when you take a breath, the air goes through your nose or mouth, through your trachea, and into your bronchial tubes. These tubes divide over and over again into smaller tubes inside your lungs. At the end of each tube is a small sac called an alveolus. Capillaries carrying blood to and from the heart surround the alveoli. It is in these capillaries that oxygen and carbon dioxide are exchanged. If you looked inside your lungs you would think they resembled a tree much more than a balloon.

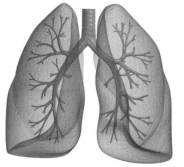

Lung with bronchial tubes

The body has been designed to protect the lungs from elements in the air that might damage them. First, hairs in the nasal passage help to filter out dust particles and other debris. Next, special tissues in the back of the throat help kill bacteria before they can enter the lungs. The

HOW BIG ARE MY LUNGS?

Purpose: To see how much air your lungs can hold

Materials: balloon, cloth tape measure

Procedure:

1. Take a deep breath and blow as much air as possible into a balloon using only one breath. If you have trouble blowing up the balloon, ask your mom or dad to blow it up for you and release the air a few times first. This will stretch the balloon making it easier to inflate.

2. After you breathe into the balloon, tie a knot in it.

3. Use a cloth tape measure to measure the circumference of the balloon and compare it with others to see who has the biggest lungs.

BREATH TEST

Purpose: To see how exercise affects our breathing rate

Materials: stopwatch

Procedure:

1. Sit still for several minutes.

2. Use a stopwatch to count how many breaths you take in one minute.

3. Exercise for five minutes by running in place or doing jumping jacks.

4. Count how many breaths you take in one minute.

5. Rest for 5 minutes and then count how many breaths you take in one minute. How did your rate of breathing change with your activities?

Conclusion: In lesson 24 you did a similar set of measurements with your pulse or heartbeat. Your heart beats faster when you exercise because your body needs more oxygen and your heart is pushing the blood around your body faster. If your blood is moving through your lungs faster, you need to get oxygen into your lungs faster, too. Therefore, you have to take more breaths when you exercise than when you are resting.

Heart & Lungs

bronchial tubes are lined with mucous that traps smaller dust particles that might pass through the nose or mouth. Tiny hairs, called **cilia**, sweep these particles out of the bronchi into the esophagus where they are eliminated in the digestive system. Finally, any particles or bacteria that do make it into the lungs are eliminated by special white blood cells that are found in the lining of the alveoli. This design by your Creator helps to keep your lungs healthy.

Many people use inhalers to treat asthma.

As we discussed earlier, keeping blood flowing continuously to get oxygen to the body is one of the most essential functions of the body. This is why one of the first things you learn in a first aid class is how to help someone who has stopped breathing. But there are several things that can interfere with your ability to breathe well. These include sickness and lung disease. When you get a cold or flu, your lungs can become irritated and produce mucus, causing you to cough. **Pneumonia** is an illness that causes fluid to settle in the lungs. **Asthma** is when the bronchial tubes swell, reducing the amount of air that can pass. All of these conditions can be treated with medication to help ease the symptoms and allow you to breathe easily again. However, some illnesses cause permanent damage to the lungs and can permanently reduce a person's breathing ability.

One of the most damaging things people do to their lungs is smoke cigarettes. Smoking causes tar to build up inside the lungs and reduces a person's ability to breathe well. Smoking also causes cancer and other diseases that can kill the smoker. God told us that our bodies are the temple of the Holy Spirit (1 Corinthians 6:19–20) and we have an obligation to take care of that temple. Therefore, we should never do anything to knowingly harm our bodies. ■

WHAT DID WE LEARN?

- How does your body keep harmful particles from entering your lungs?
- How are your lungs similar to a balloon?
- How are your lungs different from a balloon?

TAKING IT FURTHER

- What can you do to keep your lungs healthy?
- If you breathe in oxygen and breathe out carbon dioxide, how can you help someone who is not breathing by breathing into his or her lungs when you do CPR?

WORD PUZZLE

You have learned many vocabulary words in this unit. Use those vocabulary words to create your own word puzzle or word game. Once you have the puzzle or game completed, give it to your teacher or classmate to see how much they remember.

UNIT 6

Skin & Immunity

THE SKIN

Keeping your insides in

What are some of the unique things about your skin?

Words to know:

integumentary system

elastin

melanocyte

melanin

Challenge words:

carotene

albinism

BEGINNERS

You may not think that your skin is very amazing, but it is. It covers nearly every part of your body. Your skin helps to keep out things that shouldn't get into your body, like dirt and germs. Your skin also helps to keep things inside that should stay inside, like your bones, blood, and organs. The inside of your body is much wetter than the outside air, and your skin helps to keep that moisture inside your body.

Your skin does other things, too. When you get hot, your skin produces sweat that helps to cool you off. Your skin also contains millions of nerves that let you feel the world around you. Finally, your skin protects you from the harmful rays of the sun.

Your skin is stretchy and elastic, which allows you to move easily. It moves in every direction, and then goes back to its original shape. Be glad that you have such a special covering.

- What kinds of things does your skin keep out of your body?
- What kinds of things does your skin keep inside your body?
- How does your skin help you control your body temperature?
- How does your skin work together with the nervous system?

The largest organ in your body is your skin. Your skin is part of the **integumentary system**, which includes your hair and nails as well. Your skin weighs about twice as much as your brain, and it serves several functions. First, it serves as a shield to protect the rest of your body from the outside world. Your skin protects you by keeping out things that could harm you such as viruses, bacteria, and other foreign particles. It helps to protect you from hot and cold. Your skin also keeps out wind and rain and protects you from solar radiation.

Second, your skin keeps your insides in. It keeps your body from drying out by making a barrier between your moist body and the drier air. Your skin also helps you regulate your body temperature by opening and closing sweat glands, and by widening and narrowing blood vessels in your skin.

Finally, your skin works together with your nervous system as a communication network to your brain. The nerves in your skin collect information and send it to your brain continuously.

God designed your skin in amazing ways. It is stretchy and elastic, allowing you to move freely but not lose your shape. Your skin contains a substance called **elastin**, which lets your skin stretch and then contract back to its normal shape. Your skin allows your hand to grasp delicate items as easily as it grasps a hard rock. Skin is thickest on the soles of your feet and thinnest on your eyelids. It allows you to experience the whole world outside your body.

Melanocytes are cells located in the bottom layer of the skin's epidermis. These

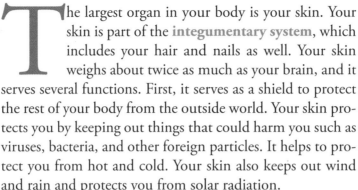

FUN FACT

Your skin secretes a substance called keratin that hardens the top layer of skin cells to make them tougher and stronger. This is the same substance that your fingernails, toenails, and hair are made from.

EXAMINING YOUR SKIN

Purpose: To observe the skin on the various parts of your body

Materials: mirror, hand lotion

Procedure:

1. Compare the color, texture, and overall appearance of the skin in each area:
   - Back of your hand
   - Fingertips
   - Bottoms of your feet
   - Forehead (use a mirror)
   - Knee

How is the skin different in each area? How is the skin the same in each area?

1. Apply lotion to part of your arm. Compare the lubricated skin with the skin on the other arm. How does lotion affect the texture and color of your skin? Your skin secretes oil that keeps your skin moist just like the lotion. Sometimes when the air is particularly dry or you wash your hands a lot, your skin becomes dry and you can help restore moisture by using lotion.

2. Examine your arm again. What do you notice besides skin? You also have tiny hairs all over your skin. The hair is thicker on some parts of the body than it is on other parts. This hair helps to keep you warm and to detect changes in your surroundings.

3. Try blowing gently across your arm. Sometimes this will cause you to get goose bumps as tiny muscles contract causing the hair to stand out from your arm.

Skin & Immunity

FUN FACT

Our lips appear red because lip skin has fewer melanocytes, allowing the red blood vessels to show through.

cells produce **melanin**, a pigment in the skin, eyes, and hair that gives them color. There are between 1,000 and 2,000 melanocytes per square millimeter of skin. They make up about 5–10% of all the cells in the skin. The difference in skin color between fair people and dark people is due not to the number of melanocytes in their skin, but to the melanocytes' level of activity. There are not different races of people, but merely people that have different facial features and different levels of melanin. All people on earth are related, having descended from the first two people—Adam and Eve. ∎

WHAT DID WE LEARN?

- What are the purposes of skin?
- How does skin help you stay healthy?
- How does skin allow you to move without getting stretched out?

TAKING IT FURTHER

- Other than skin, in what other ways does your body keep out germs?
- What skin problems might you experience in a dry climate?
- What skin problems might you experience in a very moist or humid climate?
- What are the dangers of a serious burn?

SKIN PIGMENT

The pigment melanin plays many important roles in your body. The most important role is protecting your skin from the harmful ultraviolet radiation from the sun. Melanin absorbs UV light so that it does not damage the skin. Of course, if you spend hours in strong sunlight you can still damage your skin and get a painful sunburn. When the melanin absorbs UV light, it stimulates the melanocytes to produce more melanin. This produces a suntan. A suntan is the body's natural response to increased ultraviolet light.

Melanin also protects the eyes from ultraviolet light. Melanin is found in the iris and helps determine your eye color. People with dark colored eyes have melanin that is closer to the surface, while people with lighter colored eyes have melanin that is farther from the surface of the eye.

As you learned earlier, melanin plays a role in skin color. People with fair skin have melanin primarily in the lower epidermis.

People with darker skin have more melanin in all layers of their skin because their melanocytes are more active. Some people also have carotene, an orange pigment, in their skin, which can add a somewhat yellowish tint to the skin. Also, melanin is not always evenly distributed in your skin. Have you ever seen a freckle? A freckle is an area in your skin that has a higher amount of melanin than the areas around it.

Melanin plays an important role in hair color as well. All people have two kinds of melanin in their hair: eumelanin and pheomelanin. Eumelanin is black and brown while pheomelanin is red. The amount of eumelanin in hair determines the darkness of its color. A low concentration of brown eumelanin in the hair will make it blond, whereas more brown eumelanin will give it a brown color. Much higher amounts of black eumelanin will result in black hair, and a low concentration of black eumelanin in the hair will make it gray.

Some people's bodies do not produce melanin. This condition is called albinism. Someone with albinism will have very white skin and hair, and their eyes are very pale. This condition is very rare and is a genetic condition. It is not an infectious disease. Albinism can affect animals as well as humans. Albinism is not dangerous for humans except for the increased risk of skin cancer, but it can be fatal for a wild animal that cannot conceal itself from its predators.

An albino zebra

CROSS-SECTION OF SKIN

What is below the surface?

LESSON
30

What is in each layer of skin?

Words to know:

epidermis

keratin

dermis

sebaceous gland

hair follicle

subcutaneous

Challenge words:

erector pili muscles

BEGINNERS

Your skin is made up of three layers. The outer layer forms a watertight barrier to keep things out of the body. The middle layer contains many important features. This layer contains nerves so you can feel things like pain, pressure, hot, and cold. It also contains sweat glands to help cool you off when you get too hot. It has oil glands that make oil to keep your skin soft. Finally, the middle layer can have hair. Many parts of your body have hair, not just your head. Look at your arm to see the hairs on your arm.

The innermost layer of skin contains fat cells to help keep you warm. This layer also connects your skin to your body. Your skin also has elastic fibers that allow it to stretch and move easily and then return to its original shape. You can look at the diagram of the skin on the next page and see the names of each part of the skin.

- How many layers does your skin have?

- Which layer of skin keeps water out?

- Which layer of skin has fat cells?

- Which layer of skin contains nerves?

Although the skin may seem like a simple organ, it is actually quite complex. Skin is divided into three layers: the epidermis, the dermis, and the subcutaneous tissue. The **epidermis** is the top layer. The cells on the very top of the epidermis are dead cells that are shed as they rub against clothing and other objects. Just below the dead cells are cells that have **keratin**, a substance that makes them tough and strong. This layer of cells provides the watertight barrier of the skin.

The second layer, the **dermis**, is where most of the functions of the skin take place. This layer contains sweat glands that secrete sweat to cool off the body when it gets too hot. It also contains **sebaceous glands** that secrete oil to keep the skin soft and flexible. Several types of nerve endings are also in the dermis. These include nerves to detect pain, pressure, vibration, heat, and cold. Blood vessels and **hair follicles** are in this layer. Hair grows out of hair follicles.

The innermost layer of skin is the **subcutaneous** tissue. This is a fatty layer that connects the dermis to the tissues of the body. These fat cells provide insulation to protect the body from extreme temperatures and shocks, while allowing your hand to perfectly fit around whatever it is grasping.

Your skin also contains elastic fibers called elastin, which allow your skin to stretch

SKIN WORD SEARCH

Complete the "Skin Word Search."

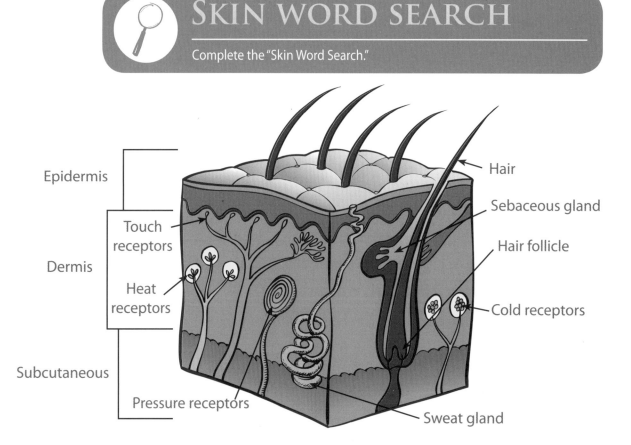

Epidermis

Dermis

Subcutaneous

Touch receptors

Heat receptors

Pressure receptors

Hair

Sebaceous gland

Hair follicle

Cold receptors

Sweat gland

Skin & Immunity

and then resume its normal shape. As people get older their elastin breaks down and the skin cannot spring back, thus it becomes more wrinkled.

Overall the skin is a very complicated organ, so, the next time you look at your skin, thank God for His great design. ■

WHAT DID WE LEARN?

- What are the three layers of skin?
- What is the purpose of the sebaceous gland?
- In which layer are most receptors located?

TAKING IT FURTHER

- Explain what happens to your skin when you pick up a pin.
- How does your skin help regulate your body temperature?

HAIR PRODUCTION

One of the more interesting functions of skin is the production of hair. Hair grows on many parts of your body including your head, arms, legs, and eyebrows. Hair in each location serves an important function. Hair on your head helps to keep heat in your body. It also helps define how you look depending on how you comb and style your hair.

Hair on your arms and many other parts of your body help you detect changes in your surroundings. As you learned in lesson 15, your hairs have nerves attached to them that detect breezes and cool temperatures. These nerves are connected to tiny muscles called the erector pili muscles. When your body feels cold, these muscles contract, causing goose bumps. This sudden movement helps to warm your body and to alert you that you need to take action to warm yourself up.

Your eyebrows and eyelashes serve to keep sweat and other substances out of your eyes. Even hair in your armpits serves a purpose. It reduces friction when you move your arms.

Hair grows from the hair follicles in your skin. People have between 100,000 and 150,000 hair follicles on their scalps. The Bible says that God cares enough about each of us that He even knows the exact number of hairs on our heads (Luke 12:7). A hair follicle is a vertical tube in the dermis. In the bottom of the follicle is the hair root. Cells in the root reproduce very quickly. They fill with keratin then die. As more cells are produced, the dead cells are pushed up. This is how hair grows. The dead cells form the shaft of the hair.

The shape of the follicle determines how the hair will look. If the follicle is round, the hair shaft will be straight and you will have straight hair. If the follicle is oval-shaped, you will have wavy hair. Sometimes hair follicles are kidney bean-shaped or very flattened. This shape of hair follicle produces very curly or kinky hair. What shape do you think your follicles are?

Hair on different parts of the body grows at different rates. On average, human hair grows about a half inch every month, but this varies from person to person. At any one time, about 90% of your hairs are growing and about 10% are resting. After a hair has grown for two to six years, it rests for about three months, and then usually falls out. So you are constantly losing hairs. You lose between 30 and 100 hairs every day. But don't worry; you won't be going bald anytime soon. Your body will grow new hairs to replace the ones that fall out.

Speaking of going bald, do some research and find out what causes baldness. Share what you find with your class or family.

FINGERPRINTS

You are unique

LESSON 31

Do you have loops, arches, or whorls on your fingers?

Words to know:

arch

loop

whorl

Challenge words:

forensic science

BEGINNERS

Look very closely at your finger tips. Do you notice the designs on each finger? Remember when you learned about friction skin in lesson 10? This special skin helps you grip things. The friction skin on your fingers forms little hills and valleys that make a pattern on each one, and the pattern on each finger is different from every other finger in the world. Each person's fingerprints are unique.

The patterns usually form one of three different types of pictures. Fingerprints can make little hills called an **arch**. They can also make curls that are called **loops**. Or the fingerprints can form a circle pattern called a **whorl**. Look at your fingerprints. Can you tell which ones make arches, loops, or whorls? Look at the pictures on the next page to help you decide. God made you special, even down to your fingerprints.

• **What are fingerprints?**

• **What are the three main pictures formed by fingerprints?**

God designed different types of skin for different parts of your body. The skin on your lips has no hair follicles and has a different color than your other skin. God also designed each person's skin to be unique. As you learned in lesson 10, you have special skin called friction skin on the palms of your hands and the bottoms of your feet. This skin has ridges and furrows that are like little hills and valleys. Friction skin helps you hold onto things with your hands and keeps your feet from slipping when you walk.

The patterns formed by these ridges and furrows are unique to each person. These patterns develop about 3–4 months before you are born and they never change throughout your lifetime. Your fingerprints are one thing that makes you different from every other person who has ever lived. Even identical twins have different fingerprints.

Although every person has unique fingerprints, fingerprints can be grouped into three different categories, as shown below. Approximately 60% of all fingerprints are loops, 35% are whorls, and 5% are arches. **Arches** are designs that enter from one side and exit on the other. **Loops** are designs that enter and exit from the same side. **Whorls** are designs that form a circular pattern. In the past, fingerprints were collected using inkpads. Today optical scanners are used to take pictures of fingerprints, then computers are used to identify prints from hundreds of thousands of prints on file. This can be accomplished very quickly with computers.

Examine your fingerprints closely and see if you can identify which type of pattern you have on each finger. Remember, God made you special, even down to your fingertips. ■

Arch

Loop

Whorl

Skin & Immunity

FINGERPRINT IDENTIFICATION

Pretend you are a police officer investigating a crime, and do the following activity.

Purpose: To collect and examine fingerprints

Materials: paper, pencil, clear tape, index cards

Procedure:

1. Trace each person's hand on a blank piece of paper and label the paper with his name.

2. Rub a pencil across a scrap piece of paper to make a very dark area about 2 inches square.

3. Have each person rub his or her fingertips, one at a time, across the dark area until the fingertip is black or dark gray. Recolor the paper as necessary to make it easy to get the prints.

4. Take a piece of clear tape and press it against the fingertip to "lift" the print.

5. Place the tape on the matching finger that was drawn on the blank paper.

6. Repeat for each finger on the hand. These pages are now your fingerprint file.

7. Now create "evidence" by lifting prints from each person and placing them on an index card.

8. Number each index card and have someone record which number matches which suspect, but don't let anyone else know.

9. Choose one card to be the guilty party and have each person try to match the evidence card to the correct page in the file. Be sure to look for arches, loops, and whorls to help you match the evidence to the right suspect.

10. After this card has been matched to a suspect, choose another card and repeat the process. See if you can match each card to the correct person.

If you would like to do some fun online sleuthing, you can learn more about being a fingerprint detective by visiting www.wonderville.ca/v1/activities/mystery/mysteryactivity.html

WHAT DID WE LEARN?

- Where can friction skin be found on your body?
- When are fingerprints formed?
- What are the three major groups of fingerprints?
- Can you identify identical twins by their fingerprints?

TAKING IT FURTHER

- What are some circumstances where fingerprints are used?
- Why do prints only occur on the hands and feet?
- Do children's fingerprints match their parents' prints?

FUN FACT

The word *forensic* comes from the Latin word that means forum. During Roman times, legal proceedings were held in the forum. Each side would present their case and the judge would decide the outcome. The person with the best forensic (forum) skills would win the case. This has led to some confusion with the use of the word forensics today. *Forensic science* involves evidence presented in court, whereas *forensic skills* usually refers to public speaking skills. A forensics club would teach speech and debate skills, not collecting and identifying of fingerprints.

Skin & Immunity

FORENSIC SCIENCE

Forensic science is the study of items related to legal proceedings. The information collected by a forensic scientist is usually used as evidence in a trial. Collecting and identifying fingerprints is only one area of forensic science. A forensic scientist might also collect shoe prints or even lip prints from a crime scene.

Forensic scientists also collect and type blood samples to use as evidence in a crime. Blood at a crime scene can tell a forensic scientist many things. Blood type can reveal if blood came from more than one person. It can tell if the blood was from the victim or the criminal. Also, a scientist can examine where and how the blood was splattered and determine what might have taken place.

A newer area of forensic science is the collection of DNA or genetic information. You will learn more about genetics and DNA in lesson 33, but it is important to know that every person has unique DNA stored in the cells of his body. So collecting some skin, hair, or blood gives the scientist a sample of the person's DNA. Careful comparison between the sample collected at the crime scene and the DNA of the suspect can yield important evidence.

Forensic scientists also collect fibers. Whenever two materials touch each other, very small fibers are left behind. These fibers can be collected and compared with clothing or other items to determine who or what may have been at the crime scene.

Finally, dental evidence is sometimes collected by forensic scientists. Each person has unique teeth. The bite patterns are unique for each person as well as the dental work that has been done. Using dental records, people can be identified by the work that has been done on their teeth.

Purpose: To practice forensics on "blood splatters"

Materials: light corn syrup, water, red food coloring, newspaper, white paper, eyedropper, "Blood Splatter Chart"

Procedure:

1. Make some sample "blood" by combining ¼ cup of light corn syrup with ¼ cup of water. Add several drops of red food coloring to this mixture. Now you are ready to start.

2. Cover the floor with newspaper and lay a sheet of white paper on top of the newspaper.

3. Fill an eyedropper with your "blood" solution.

4. Hold the dropper 2 cm above the paper and let one drop fall onto the paper.

5. Measure the diameter of the drop in millimeters and record your measurement on the "Blood Splatter Chart."

6. Next, hold the dropper at a height of 4 cm above the paper and let another drop fall onto the paper.

7. Measure and record this drop's diameter.

8. Repeat this process for all the heights listed on the chart. Replace the paper as often as necessary to avoid confusion about which drop to measure.

9. Once you have the chart completed, place a blank sheet of paper on the newspapers.

10. Have someone drop a drop of "blood" from some height between 2 cm and 100 cm without telling you that height.

11. Measure the diameter of the drop on the paper and use your chart to determine the height that you think the drop fell from.

Conclusion: This is a similar process to what a forensic scientist might go through in examining a crime scene. She must look at the pattern of blood or other liquid, and determine what direction and height it came from to help determine what actually happened at the crime scene.

THE IMMUNE SYSTEM

Keeping you healthy

LESSON
32

Words to know:

How does your body protect itself from foreign invaders?

Words to know:

immune system

lymph system

lymph

lymph nodes

antibody

thymus

bone marrow

spleen

Challenge words:

vaccination

antibiotics

BEGINNERS

Germs are everywhere! They are in the air, they are in the water, and they are in the food you eat. Thankfully, God designed your body to be able to deal with all the germs around you. The parts of your body that get rid of germs and keep you healthy make up your **immune system**.

The first part of your immune system is your skin which keeps out almost all of the germs around you. Tears in your eyes and the saliva in your mouth also help to get rid of germs and to keep them out of your body.

The second part of your immune system is called your **lymph system**. This is a collection of vessels, similar to blood vessels, which carry a clear liquid to all the tissues of your body, collecting germs to be taken to areas in the body where they can be destroyed. The third part of your immune system is the white blood cells in your blood. These cells are specially designed to destroy any invaders in the body.

Even with all these defenses, sometimes germs get through and you become sick. When this happens, your body produces many more white blood cells and they work until they kill all the germs. You may feel sick for a little while, but the immune system God gave you will fight off the sickness.

- How does your skin help to keep you from getting sick?

- How does the lymph system help to keep you healthy?

- How do white blood cells help to keep you from getting sick?

Germs are everywhere! They are in the air, they are in the water, and they are in the food we eat. Viruses and bacteria, commonly called germs, are constantly trying to enter our bodies. If germs get into your body and begin to multiply, they can make you sick by producing toxins that cause inflammation or which damage or destroy cells. Thankfully, God designed our bodies to be able to deal with the multitude of germs around us. Your **immune system** works to keep germs from making you sick.

There are several ways that your body deals with germs. The first and most important thing your body does is to try to keep germs out of your body. Your skin is the largest part of your immune system and is the first line of defense against germs. As long as your skin is not broken, germs cannot pass through your skin. Also, your skin produces anti-bacterial substances that keep bacteria from growing on your skin.

But your skin cannot keep out all germs. Germs can enter through your nose, mouth, and eyes, as well as through cuts in your skin. Tears in your eyes and saliva in your mouth both contain enzymes which help to break down bacteria before they have a chance to do any harm. Also, mucus in your nasal passages and throat trap particles, including bacteria and viruses, so they can be eliminated in the stomach.

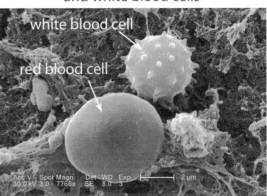

Electron micrograph of red and white blood cells

Even with these very effective measures, sometimes germs get inside your body and start to reproduce. So there is more to your immune system than just skin, tears, and mucus. Your lymph and circulatory systems are the other major parts of your immune system. The **lymph system** is similar to your circulatory system. It consists of vessels throughout your body that carry **lymph**, a clear liquid, to all the cells and tissues. This liquid picks up many germs and the **lymph nodes**, bean-shaped nodules containing white blood cells, filter them out. The lymph system can be considered the second line of defense against germs.

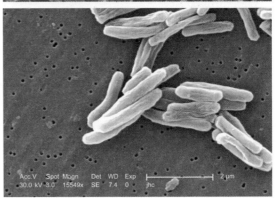

Electron micrograph of *Tuberculosis* bacteria

The third line of defense is in your circulatory system. White blood cells play a major role in defending against viruses and bacteria. There are many different types of white blood cells, but most of them serve a similar purpose. White blood cells detect any foreign object in the blood and quickly surround and eliminate it. White blood cells also generate proteins called antibodies.

LEARNING ABOUT IMMUNITIES

Sometimes our immune systems do not work correctly. Do some research on allergies, diabetes, and rheumatoid arthritis. These are all conditions in which the immune system is malfunctioning.

Antibodies are unique and can only attack one kind of bacteria or virus. Antibodies bind bacteria and help the white blood cells eliminate bacteria.

Other parts of your body play important roles in the immune system as well. An organ near your heart called the **thymus** produces specialized white blood cells called T-cells. **Bone marrow**, material in the center of long bones, produces most other white blood cells. And your **spleen** works as a filter for your blood and eliminates many of the germs that are not eliminated in other parts of the immune system. Together your skin, lymph system, and circulatory system, as well as the parts just mentioned, form a very effective defense system to help keep you healthy.

Sometimes, however, all of these defenses are not enough and bacteria or viruses are still able to enter your body, reproduce, and make you sick. This is when your immune system kicks into high gear and really starts producing white blood cells and antibodies to overtake the invaders. Eventually your immune system overcomes the enemy and you get well if everything is working correctly. ■

WHAT DID WE LEARN?

- What are the major parts of the immune system?
- What are the two major types of "germs" that make us sick?
- How do tears and mucus help fight germs?

TAKING IT FURTHER

- Why are a fever and the itchiness from a mosquito bite both indications that your immune system is working?

HELPING OUR IMMUNE SYSTEM

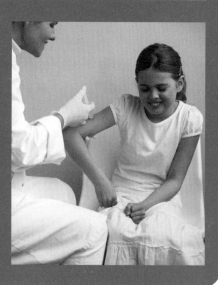

Vaccinations are a way that scientists have found to help stimulate your immune system to keep you from catching many of the most dangerous diseases. Do some research and find the answers to these questions.

- What is a vaccine?
- How do vaccines work?
- Who developed the first vaccinations?
- What kind of diseases do vaccinations work against?
- How long do vaccinations last?

Antibiotics are another way that doctors help your immune system. Do some more research and find the answers to these questions.

- What are antibiotics?
- How were antibiotics discovered?
- What are antibiotics used for?
- What are some diseases that are treated with antibiotics?

GENETICS

Why you look like you do

LESSON 33

How does DNA make your eyes brown?

Words to know:

genes

dominant gene

Challenge words:

DNA

double helix

deoxyribose

base pairs

adenine

thymine

guanine

cytosine

chromosome

mutation

BEGINNERS

You may look a lot like your brothers and sisters, but your friend or neighbor probably looks very different from you. This is because the information that makes you look the way you do came to you from your mother and father, not from your friend or neighbor. This information is stored in the **genes** in the cells of your body.

This information tells your body what color of eyes and hair you will have and how dark your skin will be. If your parents both have blue eyes, you are likely to have blue eyes, too. If one parent has blue eyes and the other has brown eyes, you could have either color. The "stronger" gene will decide what color your eyes will be.

All the information on how human bodies should be made was placed in the genes of the very first man and woman, Adam and Eve, when God created them. That information has been passed down from parent to child ever since creation.

- **Where is the information stored that tells what you will look like?**
- **Where did the information in your genes come from?**
- **Where did the original information come from for Adam's and Eve's genes?**

Have you ever noticed brothers or sisters often look alike? And children usually resemble their parents. But you may look very different from your friend or neighbor. This is because how you look, and a lot of other things about your body, are determined by something called genes, and genes are something you inherit from your parents.

Genes are tiny bits of information contained in the DNA of each cell in your body. Half of your genes came from your mother and half came from your father. This information tells your body what color your hair and eyes should be, how dark your skin will be, if you can curl your tongue, if your ear lobes are attached to your face, and thousands of other things about you.

What if your mom has blue eyes and your dad has brown eyes? What color will your eyes be? Some genes are dominant—they are "stronger"—so the **dominant gene** will determine your eye color. Brown eyes are dominant over blue, so you would probably have brown eyes. However, if one of your dad's parents (your grandparents) had blue eyes, your dad could pass on a blue eye gene to you and you might have blue eyes. But you would have a better chance of having brown eyes than blue ones.

God created Adam and Eve with a wide variety of genes. They had information for many different eye colors, hair colors, skin shades, etc., so their children could have looked very different from each other. Some of that information was lost as most of the people on earth died in the Great Flood, but the wide variety we see in people today was preserved in the genes of Noah and his family.

Since identical twins come from a single egg, they have the same genetic information.

After the confusion of languages at the Tower of Babel, people began to spread throughout the earth by family groups. Since these groups became isolated from each other, the variety of the genes in one area became smaller. So some people had information for some traits and not for others. People in a particular area shared certain traits and adapted to the conditions where they lived or moved to places that better suited them. Ultimately, we see that the groups that went to Africa ended up with mostly darker skin, while the people that went to Southeast Asia had mostly dark hair, etc. Still, all people have descended from Noah and his family (and thus from Adam and Eve) and therefore we are all special creations of God created in His image. ■

GENETICS QUIZ

Get a copy of "Genetics Quiz" and follow the instructions to see which traits you inherited from each of your parents.

DNA

God made each person unique. Your genetic code is like no one else's. But what exactly is this genetic code? All of the information needed to make a human being is stored in a very long molecule called **DNA**, or deoxyribonucleic acid. In 1953 James Watson and Francis Crick were the first to accurately describe the structure of DNA. They showed that DNA is a ladder-like structure with sides and rungs. This ladder is then twisted and compressed. This structure is called a **double helix**.

The sides of the DNA ladder consist of sugar molecules, called **deoxyribose**, alternating with phosphate molecules. The rungs of the ladder are made up of pairs of chemicals called bases or **base pairs**. There are four kinds of bases that can be used to build the DNA ladder: **adenine** (A), **thymine** (T), **guanine** (G), and **cytosine** (C). Two bases connect together to form a rung, but only certain bases can be paired together. An A will

always be paired with a T and a G will always be paired with a C. The shapes of the base molecules prevent them from pairing with the wrong bases.

Now that you understand the basic structure of the DNA molecule, you can begin to understand how this molecule contains information. If you stretched out a molecule of DNA so it looks like a ladder and looked at the base pairs from top to bottom you would get a list of letters. For example

the first four rungs might be AT, TA, GC, GC. The pattern of bases provides information to the cells of your body. If the pattern were different, it would tell your body to do something different.

DNA is divided into sections called genes. Each gene in your body tells something about you, such as your hair color, height, or ability to curl your tongue. A gene contains about 100,000 base pairs, or rungs on the ladder, and each pair has to be in a

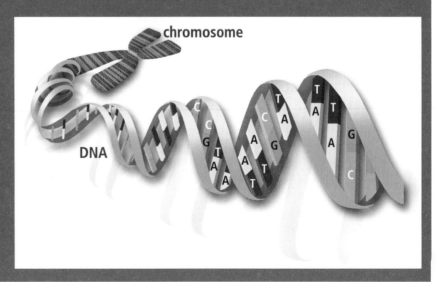

specific order. Now that's a lot of information.

No one knows exactly how many genes are in the human body. It is estimated that there are between 20,000 and 25,000 genes. The Human Genome Project is a group of scientists working to map the complete human DNA sequence. When they are done analyzing their data, we should know how many genes are needed to make a human body.

Thousands of genes are connected together to form a strand of DNA. A complete strand of DNA is called a chromosome. The cells in the human body contain 23 pairs of chromosomes for a total of 46 chromosomes. These chromosomes are stored in the nucleus of each cell. When the body needs information from the DNA, the correct chromosome is unwound and the section containing the information is passed through a special mechanism in the cell that reads the sequence of base pairs to get the information. Then the DNA is zipped back together and rewound. This is a very efficient way to store information.

If the information stored in the DNA were to get messed up, the body might not be able to do something that it should. This is why God created our bodies with two sets of chromosomes.

One set is given to the baby by the mother, and the second set is given to the baby by the father. With two sets of code, it is unlikely that a mistake in the code would occur at the same location in both codes. Occasionally a problem will occur in the same location in both codes, and this usually results in a birth defect or a disease in the child. These mistakes are called mutations and are almost always harmful to the person. Evolutionists claim that millions of mutations in genetic codes are what has caused life to evolve; however, beneficial mutations are practically unheard of; they are almost always harmful to the organism, and do not provide any new information.

Purpose: To better understand how DNA works by building a model

Materials: "DNA Puzzle Pieces," scissors, tape

(If you have an actual 3-D model you can follow the directions included with your model to build the DNA strand.)

Procedure:

1. Make several copies of the "DNA Puzzle Pieces" and cut them out.

2. Tape the correct base pairs together. Be sure to only tape A's and T's together, and C's and G's together.

3. Once you have several pairs put together, arrange them vertically on the table to form a ladder.

4. Tape the sides of the ladder together. This will represent a very small section of one gene.

GREGOR MENDEL

1823–1884

Gregor Mendel was the first person to trace the characteristics of successive generations of living things. In other words, he was the first to show that many traits are passed on by parents to their children.

Gregor Mendel was the second child of Anton and Rosine Mendel, farmers in Brunn, Moravia (a part of the Austro-Hungarian Empire at that time).

Today, as we look back at his work, it would be easy to think of him as a world-renowned scientist of his day, but this is not the way it was. Gregor had done very well in school and his family wanted him to pursue higher education but they did not have much money. So Gregor entered a monastery to continue his education. There he also worked as a teacher and taught natural science to high school students.

Gregor Mendel had a real love for nature. He seemed to really enjoy his work. He said that he crossed different characteristics of peas over several generations just "for the fun of the thing." His initial work was inspired as he took frequent walks in the monastery's gardens. One day he found a plant with unusual characteristics. He moved it next to some other plants of the same type to see what would happen to the offspring. He found that some of the next generation of plants exhibited the unusual characteristics. This simple test gave him the idea of heredity. He also thought that some traits were dominant over others and were more likely to be inherited.

Mendel decided to test his theories on peas. So he spent the next seven years cross-breeding peas before he was able to prove the laws of inheritance. From this work, Mendel derived the basic laws of heredity, showing that hereditary factors do not combine, but are passed intact. This means, for example, that if one parent plant has rounded seeds and the other has wrinkled seeds, the offspring will have either rounded or wrinkled seeds, but not something in between.

He also showed that one parent gives half the genes, or hereditary factors, with the other half coming from the other parent. And he proved that some characteristics are dominant over others. Finally, Mendel showed that different offspring of the same set of parents would receive different sets of hereditary factors. Two children from the same parents will not look identical (with the exception of identical twins who both developed from the same fertilized egg).

Because of Mendel's work, we now know that many diseases are inherited and can be traced along ancestral lines. This information can help unborn children by giving the doctors help in knowing what to look for. With this information today, some serious conditions can be treated before the baby is even born.

Mendel performed his experiments at about the same time that Darwin was developing his theory of evolution. Unlike Darwin, who based most of his theory on guesses and suppositions, Mendel performed his research very carefully and recorded exactly what he saw. He was able to demonstrate each of his ideas by showing the data from his experiments. In fact, the results Mendel achieved went against Darwin's idea of selective breeding resulting in new kinds of animals.

Mendel was able to demonstrate that the genes from the parents determine what the offspring will look like. Therefore, he showed that one kind of plant or animal will always produce that same kind of plant or animal. Evolutionists have had to "update" Darwin's theory by saying that mutations (mistakes) in the genes are what caused the changes from one kind of animal to another. However, all mutations that have been observed have only resulted in a loss of genetic information, not a gain as would be required for one creature to change into another kind of creature.

Although Mendel was not recognized as a great scientist in his lifetime, his work has had a profound impact on science today. Mendel's love for nature, his awareness of small differences around him, and his careful approach to experiments enabled him to make many important discoveries that laid the foundation for the field of genetics today.

LESSON

34

Now that you have learned about each of the major systems of the human body, it is time to put what you have learned all together to better understand how your body works. Each system cannot function independently. They all have different but complementary jobs to do. They all work together.

For example, the brain and the rest of the nervous system control all of the other systems. Without your brain, nothing else would work. Your digestive system works together with your circulatory system to provide energy to your body. Your respiratory system works with your circulatory system to move oxygen and carbon dioxide around your body. God has created a marvelous and complex body for you so you can enjoy the world He made. ■

BODY POSTER

Purpose: To make a full-size drawing of your body systems

Materials: large piece of paper, pen or marker, anatomy guide

Procedure:

1. Lie down on a piece of large paper such as a roll of newsprint.

2. Have someone trace around your body with a pen or marker.

3. Draw in each of the systems studied in this unit. You might draw the nervous system on the left side of the body and the skeletal and muscular systems on the right side. Add the circulatory system to both sides.

4. Draw the lungs and heart on separate pieces of paper and tape them on the body so that they can be lifted to see what is underneath. Do the same thing for the digestive system.

5. Explain to your teacher or parent how each of these systems works individually and how the systems work together.

Skin & Immunity

WHAT DID WE LEARN?

- Name the eight body systems you have learned about.

- How do some of the different systems work together?

TAKING IT FURTHER

- What other systems can you think of that are in your body but were not discussed in this book?

- How do you see evidence of God the Creator in the design of the human body?

BODY RESEARCH

Choose one part of the body that you would like to know more about. Research that part and make a poster explaining what you learned. Make this presentation as detailed as your teacher or parent wants.

Skin & Immunity

CONCLUSION

Appreciating the human body

LESSON 35

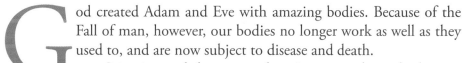

God created Adam and Eve with amazing bodies. Because of the Fall of man, however, our bodies no longer work as well as they used to, and are now subject to disease and death.

Scientists and doctors are learning more about the human body every day. And the more they learn, the more they are amazed at the complexity and beauty of its design. There is no way that such complexity and organization could come about through naturalistic evolution. No, God created us.

Not only did God create your wonderful body, but He also cares deeply for you. Read the following Bible verses with your teacher or your mom or dad. Discuss the kind of relationship God wants to have with each of us.

- Matthew 10:29–31
- Isaiah 44:24
- Psalm 24:1
- Psalm 139:13–18

Using a concordance, look up verses in the Bible that talk about the body. What does the Bible say about the body? Discuss these verses with your teacher or parents and write a thank you note to God, thanking Him for making you special. ■

Skin & Immunity

GLOSSARY

Alveoli   Sacs where exchange of gases takes place in the lungs (singular is *alveolus*)

Amplitude   How high waves are; in sound this determines loudness

Antibodies   Proteins that attack and destroy invading substances

Arteries   Blood vessels that carry blood away from the heart

Asthma   Swelling of the bronchial tubes

Atrium   Upper chamber in the heart that receives blood (plural is *atria*)

Auditory canal   Opening of the ear

Ball and socket joint   Moves in two planes, rotates in place

Bicep and tricep   Muscle pair in upper arm

Bicuspids   Bumpy teeth for grinding, next to canine teeth

Bone marrow   Material in the center of long bones that produces blood cells

Brain stem   Connection between the rest of the brain and the spinal cord, regulates automatic functions

Bronchi/Bronchial tubes   Tubes entering the lungs

Capillaries   Blood vessels that connect arteries and veins

Carbohydrates   Sugars and starches

Carpals   Bones of the wrist

Cartilage   Smooth, slippery material forming cushion between bones

Cell membrane   Protective shell or "skin" of the cell

Cell   Smallest part of the human body that can function on its own

Central nervous system   Brain and spinal cord

Cerebellum   Lower part of the brain, controlling balance and muscle movement

Cerebral cortex   Outermost layer of the cerebrum

Cerebrum   Upper part of the brain, controlling thought and memory

Cilia   Tiny hairs covering many body tissues

Circulatory system   System of heart, blood, and blood vessels that carry oxygen and nutrients throughout the body.

Clavicle   Collarbone

Cochlea   Fluid-filled part of the ear that changes vibrations to electrical signals

Cones   Special cells in the retina to detect color

Cornea   Front of the eye

Corpus callosum   Large bundle of nerves connecting two sides of the cerebrum

Cranium   Skull

Cuspids/Canine teeth   Pointed teeth for tearing

Cytoplasm   Liquid inside the cell

Dermis   Middle layer of skin containing nerves, sweat glands, and other functions

Diaphragm   Muscle below lungs that expands the chest cavity when it contracts

Digestive system   System of organs that removes nutrients from food you eat

Dominant gene   "Stronger" gene, or predominant characteristic that is passed down from parent to child

Elastin   Elastic-like fibers that allow skin to stretch

Ellipsoid joint   Moves in two planes without rotating

Enzymes   chemicals that help with the digestion process

Epidermis   Top layer of skin

Esophagus   Tube connecting your mouth with your stomach

Femur   Large bone in upper leg

Fibrin   Stringy substance that helps form scabs

Fibula   Smaller bone in lower leg

Flat bones   Scapula, cranium, ribs, and pelvis

Frequency   How close waves are together; in sound this determines pitch

Friction skin   Ridged skin found on feet and hands, for gripping

Genes   Tiny bits of information contained in the body's cells, stored in DNA

Gliding joint   Bones slide over each other

Gluteus maximus   Muscle in rear

Hair follicle   Area in skin where hair is formed

Malleus, incus, and stapes   Tiny bones in the middle ear

Hemoglobin   Chemical in red blood cells that turns bright red in the presence of oxygen

Hinge joint   Moves in only one direction

Hippocampus   Part of the brain that stores and retrieves short-term memory

Humerus   Bone in upper arm

Immune system   System of organs that work together to fight off infection

Incisors   Sharp straight teeth for biting

Integumentary system   System of organs including the skin, nails, and hair

Involuntary muscles   Muscles that are controlled without conscious thought

Iris   Colored part of the eye, controls size of pupil

Irregular bones   Bones that don't fit into any other category for shape

Keratin   Substance that makes skin tough

Large intestine   Tube where water is removed from unusable material

Larynx   Voice box

Lens   Part of the eye that focuses the image

Long bones   Arm and leg bones

Loops, whorls, and arches   Patterns formed by fingerprints

Lymph nodes   Bean-shaped organs in the lymph system containing white blood cells

Lymph system   System of vessels and lymph nodes that help eliminate invading substances

Lymph   Clear liquid in the lymph system that collects germs to be carried to the lymph nodes for elimination

Mandible   Jawbone

Medulla oblongata   Lowest part of the brain stem

Melanin   Pigment cells in the skin

Melanocytes   Cells which produce melanin

Metacarpals   Bones in the hand

Mitochondria   Break down nutrients to provide energy for the cell

Molars   Large bumpy teeth for grinding, in back of mouth

Muscular system   System of muscles that move the bones and other parts of the body

Nervous system   System of nerves that control the body

Neuron   Nerve cell

Nucleus   Brain of the cell

Optic nerve   Nerve that transmits image to the brain

Organ   Many tissues working together to perform a function

Patella   Kneecap

Pectoral   Muscles in upper chest

Peripheral nervous system   Nerves and other sensory organs

Phalanges   Small bones in your fingers and toes

Pharynx   Back of the throat

Pituitary gland   Part of the brain that controls growth

Pivot joint   Rotates only

Plaque   Sticky substance that builds up on teeth

Plasma   Yellowish liquid that transports blood cells

Platelets   Cells that help to close a wound

Pneumonia   Illness causing fluid in the lungs

Pulmonary artery   Artery carrying blood from the heart to the lungs

Pulmonary veins   Veins carrying blood from the lungs to the heart

Pupil   Opening in the eye that allows light to enter

Radius   Bone in the lower arm on the side with your thumb

Red blood cells   Cells that carry oxygen and nutrients to the body

Reflex   Automatic reaction that does not require a signal to go to the brain

Respiratory system   System of organs including the lungs whose main function is to get oxygen to the blood

Retina   Back of the eye that detects the image

Rods   Special cells in the retina to detect differences in light

Saddle joint   Moves in two planes, shaped like a saddle

Scapula   Shoulder blade

Sebaceous gland   Gland in the skin that secretes oil

Short bones   Bones of the fingers, toes, hands, and feet

Skeletal system   System of bones that provides strength and gives the body its general shape and size

Small intestine   Tube where nutrients are absorbed

Smooth muscle   Muscles that line the digestive tract and other internal organs

Spleen   Organ that filters dangerous organisms from the blood

Sternum   Bone in central chest connecting ribs

Stomach   Organ where food is broken down into smaller molecules

Subcutaneous   Lowest layer of skin, connecting skin to the body tissues

Tendon   Cord-like structure connecting muscles to bones

Thalamus   Part of the brain that routes messages within the brain

Thymus   Organ producing special white blood cells called T-cells

Tibia   Larger bone in the lower leg

Tissue   Many cells working together to perform a function

Trachea   Tube leading to the lungs

Trapezius   Muscles in upper back

Ulna   Bone in the lower arm on the side away from your thumb

Vacuole   Food storage area in the cell

Veins   Blood vessels that carry blood toward the heart

Ventricle   Lower chamber in the heart that pushes out blood

Vertebrae   Bones in the spine

Villi   Small finger-like projections inside the small intestine that absorb nutrients

Voluntary muscles   Muscles that move when you actively think about movement

White blood cells   Cells that help fight infection

CHALLENGE GLOSSARY

Adenine   Base used in DNA, must be paired with thymine

Albinism   Condition where the body does not produce melanin

Antibiotics   Chemicals that inhibit the growth of bacteria and other microorganisms

Antigens   Identification tags on cells

Appendicular skeleton   Outer bones including arms, legs, hips, shoulders, feet, and hands

Aqueous humor   Liquid between the cornea and the lens

Axial skeleton   Central bones including skull, face, neck, spine, and ribs

Axon   Part of the neuron that carries signal away from the cell body

Base pair   Two bases connected together to form a rung of the DNA molecule

Bile   Chemicals produced by the liver and stored in the gall bladder to be released into the small intestine and used for digestion

Blood pressure   Pressure placed on the walls of the blood vessels

Blood type   Determined by the absence or presence of certain antigens in the blood

Braille   System of raised dots to represent letters and other symbols

Cardiac muscle tissue   Tissue of the heart

Carotene   Orange pigment

Cellular respiration   Combination of oxygen with food molecules to release the energy

Cementum   Material next to root that secures tooth in the jaw

Chromosome   A complete strand of DNA

Collagen   Flexible protein that builds the structure of bones

Compound fracture   One in which the bone punctures the skin

Connective tissue   Connects body parts

Crown   Visible part of the tooth

Cytosine   Base used in DNA, must be paired with guanine

DNA   Deoxyribonucleic acid, molecule containing genetic information

Dendrite   Part of the neuron that receives input

Dentin   Bonelike material surrounding pulp of the tooth

Deoxyribose   Sugar molecule forming the sides of the DNA molecule

Diastolic pressure   Blood pressure when the heart is as rest

Double helix   Shape of DNA; ladder that is twisted and compacted

Enamel   Hard protective covering on teeth

Endocrine system   Produces hormones

Epithelial tissue   Lines all body parts

Erector pili muscles   Tiny muscles in the skin attached to hairs

Eustachian tube   Opening between the middle ear and the throat

Excretory system   Removes wastes from the body

External respiration   Exchange of gases in the lungs

Forensic science   Study of items used in legal proceedings

Fracture   A break in a bone

Gastric juice   Enzymes and other chemicals secreted by the lining of the stomach

Gingiva   Gums

Guanine   Base used in DNA, must be paired with cytosine

Gustatory receptor cells   Cells that react with food molecules to produce electrical signals

Hormones   Chemical messengers to regulate body functions

Internal respiration   Exchange of gases between blood cells and tissue cells

Interneuron/Association neuron   Nerve cell that interprets input and generates output

Kidneys   Main organs of the excretory system

Ligament   Flexible cord-like material that connects bones together

Motor neuron   Nerve cell that carries a signal from the brain to a muscle

Muscle tissue   Contracts, for movement

Mutation   A mistake in the genetic code

Myelin   Material produced by the Schwann cells that provides insulation

Neck   Part of tooth entering the gums

Nerve tissue   Controls body activities

Occlusion   Correct teeth and jaw alignment or normal bite

Odorants   Light molecules that produce smell

Olfactory hairs   Dendrites of the nerves in the nasal cavity that chemically react with smell molecules

Orthodontics   The dental practice of straightening teeth and correcting jaw alignment

Pancreatic juice   Enzymes and other chemicals produced by the pancreas for digestion

Papillae   Taste buds

Periodontal ligament   Fiber between cementum and jawbone material

Pulp   Center of tooth containing nerves and blood vessels

Reproductive system   Produces children

Respiration   The exchange of oxygen and carbon dioxide

Retainer   Device to hold teeth in proper position

Root canals   Channels containing blood vessels in the tooth

Root   Part of tooth anchoring the tooth in the jaw

Salivary amylase   Enzyme that breaks down starch molecules

Schwann cells   Cells that cover and insulate the axon

Semicircular canals   Fluid-filled tubes that help determine balance

Sensory neuron   Nerve cell that receives input and carries it toward the brain

Simple fracture   One in which the bone does not puncture the skin

Smooth muscle tissue   Tissue designed for long strong contractions

Sodium bicarbonate   Chemical produced by pancreas to neutralize stomach acid

Striated muscle tissue   Skeletal muscle tissue with striped appearance

Synovial fluid   Slippery fluid in the joint to facilitate smooth movement

Systolic pressure   Blood pressure when the ventricles of the heart contract

Thymine   Base used in DNA, must be paired with adenine

Universal donor   Blood type that can be donated to all other types

Universal recipient   Blood type that can receive all other types

Uterus   Womb

Vaccination   Injection of a substance that stimulates the immune system against a certain disease

Vitreous humor   Jelly-like substance in the middle of the eyeball

INDEX